FIFTY GREAT AMERICAN SILENT FILMS
1912–1920:

A PICTORIAL SURVEY

Anthony Slide &
Edward Wagenknecht

Dover Publications, Inc., New York

*To the memory of the great screen
players of the teens, in particular
Hobart Bosworth, Robert Harron,
Florence LaBadie, and Florence Turner*

By Anthony Slide
Early American Cinema (1970)
The Griffith Actresses (1973)
The Idols of Silence (1976)
The Big V (1976)
Early Women Directors (1977)
Aspects of American Film History Prior to 1920
(1978)

By Edward Wagenknecht
The Movies in the Age of Innocence (1962)
Seven Daughters of the Theater (1964)
Merely Players (1966)
As Far as Yesterday (1968)
etc. etc.

By Edward Wagenknecht and Anthony Slide
The Films of D. W. Griffith (1975)

Published in Canada by General Publishing Company, Ltd., 30
Lesmill Road, Don Mills, Toronto, Ontario.
Published in the United Kingdom by Constable and Company,
Ltd., 10 Orange Street, London WC2H 7 EG.

*Fifty Great American Silent Films, 1912–1920: A Pictorial
Survey* is a new work, first published by Dover Publications, Inc.,
in 1980.

International Standard Book Number: 0-486-23985-3
Library of Congress Catalog Card Number: 80-65178

Manufactured in the United States of America
Dover Publications, Inc.
180 Varick Street
New York, N.Y. 10014

PREFACE

This book covers fifty American feature films, arranged chronologically in the order of their release, from the 1912–1920 period, which saw the real emergence of this type of film.

We do not claim that these are "the fifty greatest films" of the period. We do claim that they are broadly representative. There are films here which one or the other or both of us love very much, and there are others which one or the other or both dislike. We agree, however, that every film included has either historical or aesthetic value or both.

In a sense, this volume is a companion to the same authors' *The Films of D. W. Griffith* (Crown Publishers, 1975), in which all the feature films of that master were covered in greater detail than has been possible here, along with general, overall consideration of his Biographs. For this reason, only Griffith's three very greatest films—*The Birth of a Nation, Intolerance,* and *Broken Blossoms*—have been treated here.

The volume closes with Charles Chaplin's *The Kid,* which was not shown until January, 1921. But it was produced in 1920, and, except for the greatly inferior *Tillie's Punctured Romance,* which starred not him but Marie Dressler, it was Chaplin's first long film. His vogue, built up in short films, was one of the two or three outstanding cinematic phenomena of our period, and we felt that it would be absurd to publish this book with no Chaplin in it.

Anthony Slide is responsible for all the credits. Edward Wagenknecht wrote most of the synopses. Both writers have contributed to the captions. All the historical-critical commentaries have been signed (with italic initials).

For the use of films and stills, and for other favors, we are indebted to the following, to all of whom it is a pleasure to express our gratitude:

The Academy of Motion Picture Arts and Sciences
The British Film Institute (Patricia Coward)
Robert Cushman
Miss Claire DuBrey
Tom Fulbright
George Eastman House (George Pratt)
Miss Lillian Gish
Robert Gitt
Miss Ethel Grandin
The Museum of Modern Art Film Library (Mary Corliss)
Jack Spears
Herb Sterne
Miss Blanche Sweet
The Wisconsin Center for Theatre Research (Susan Dalton)

We are again deeply indebted to Robert Cushman, who made the majority of the prints for us. Our debt to him in connection with the four Mary Pickford films is especially great.

A. S.   E. W.

CONTENTS

FROM THE MANGER TO THE CROSS

A Kalem production. World premiere: Queen's Hall, London, October 3, 1912. U.S. premiere: Wanamaker's Auditorium, New York, October 14, 1912. 5 reels. (Reedited and reissued in 1938 with music, commentary, and sound effects by the Reverend Brian Hession.)

Director: Sidney Olcott. Screenplay: Gene Gauntier. Photography: George K. Hollister. Scenic Artist: Allen Farnham.

CAST: R. Henderson Bland (*The Christ*); Gene Gauntier (*The Virgin Mary*); Percy Dyer (*The Boy Christ*); Alice Hollister (*Mary Magdalene*); Helen Lindroth (*Martha*); Jack J. Clark (*John*); J. P. McGowan (*Andrew*); Robert Vignola (*Judas*); Sidney Baber (*Lazarus*).

SYNOPSIS: This pictorial biography of Jesus includes his birth at Bethlehem, the flight to Egypt, the return to Nazareth, the visit to Jerusalem when Jesus was twelve, the calling of the disciples, the turning of water to wine, the raising of Lazarus, the extension of forgiveness to the woman who was a sinner, and the events of the Passion—the Last Supper, the agony in Gethsemane, the trial, and the Crucifixion.

COMMENTARY: Though Vitagraph's five-reel *Life of Moses* dates back to 1909-10, "features" before 1912 were largely two- and three-reelers, and it was not until about 1915 that the five-reeler became the staple of the ordinary film program. Most of Kalem's films were one-reelers; the firm began in 1907, and for the first three years they did not even have a studio; it is not surprising then that they should have made a virtue of necessity by turning out so many local-color films (as in their pictures about the Georgia "crackers") and action films (as in their Civil War items). But it does seem oddly ironical that their one five-reeler, which they had never wished to make at all, should now be practically the only production by which they are remembered.

Passion Plays go back to the very beginnings of film history, but the only one many filmgoers could have remembered at the time *From the Manger to the Cross* was first shown must have been the three-reel Pathé of 1907. Kalem's first excursions abroad were to Ireland in 1910 and 1911, where they made, among other things, three-reel productions of such Dion Boucicault stage works as *The Colleen Bawn* and *Arrah-na-Pogue;* these pictures, which caused their makers to be facetiously dubbed "The O'Kalems," were highly rated in their time, and the stills look very good even today.

From the Manger to the Cross was made in Egypt and Palestine, apparently on the initiative of director Sidney Olcott and Kalem's highly competent and ambitious leading actress and scenarist Gene Gauntier, without authorization from the front office. It was phenomenally successful, especially in England, where it was warmly praised by both Dean Inge and the Bishop of London. But both Olcott and Miss Gauntier were so disappointed by the attitude of their employers that they left Kalem, and with their departure the great days were over.

There was something odd about this film from the beginning. Gene Gauntier claimed to have conceived the idea in delirium while recovering from sunstroke, and Olcott engaged R. Henderson Bland over the telephone to play The Christ in a silent film because he liked his voice!

Seen today, *From the Manger to the Cross* seems more impressive in the more intimate scenes than in its crowd effects. One wonders why the Resurrection was omitted. In view of the audience to which the film was directed, rationalistic considerations can hardly be supposed to apply. Was Olcott perhaps merely being faithful to an excellent title, which had been adopted to differentiate the production from other Passion Plays? Or was he deterred by the difficulty of staging a Resurrection scene? (It must be admitted that many such are more comic than awe-inspiring.) Evidently some audiences found the omission unsatisfactory, for an unidentified hand has spliced the Resurrection episode from another film onto the end of the print of *From the Manger to the Cross* now at Eastman House. (*E. W.*)

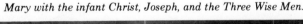

Mary with the infant Christ, Joseph, and the Three Wise Men.

Above: *The blind beggar healed. The second woman from the right is Mary Magdalene.* Below: *The scourging of Christ.*

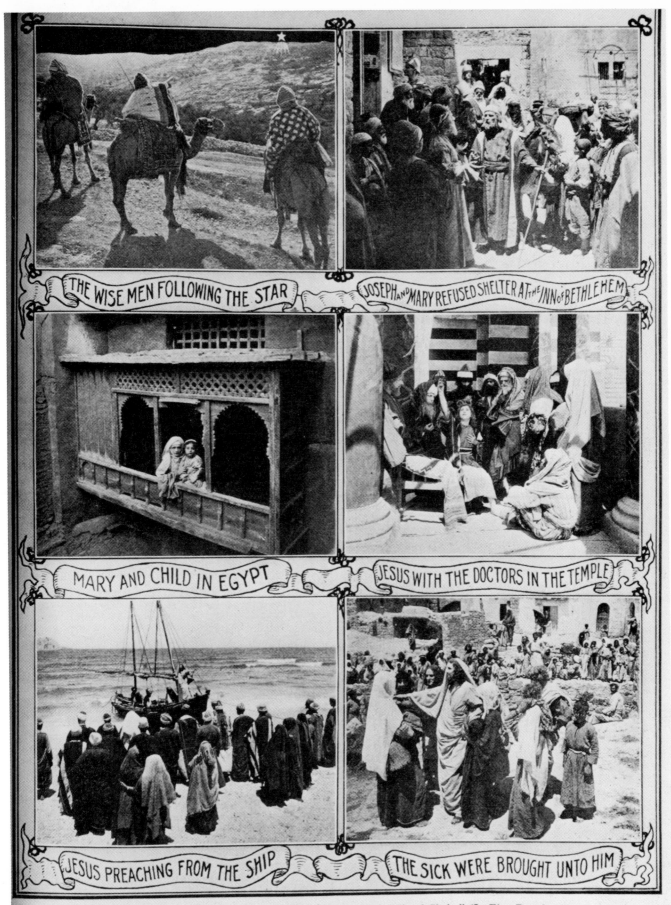

THE WISE MEN FOLLOWING THE STAR

JOSEPH AND MARY REFUSED SHELTER AT THE INN OF BETHLEHEM

MARY AND CHILD IN EGYPT

JESUS WITH THE DOCTORS IN THE TEMPLE

JESUS PREACHING FROM THE SHIP

THE SICK WERE BROUGHT UNTO HIM

Scenes from the Kalem Feature Production "The Life of Christ" (In Five Parts).

3

THE COUNT OF MONTE CRISTO

A Famous Players Film Company production. Released November 1, 1913. 5 reels.

Presented by Daniel Frohman. Director and Photography: Edwin S. Porter. Screenplay: Hampton Del Ruth (based on the stage play by Charles Fechter and the novel by Alexandre Dumas).

(*The Count of Monte Cristo* has been filmed many times, in particular in 1908 by Selig, in 1922 by William Fox, and in 1934 by Reliance.)

CAST: James O'Neill (*Edmund Dantes*).

SYNOPSIS: Between book covers, on the stage and on film, Dumas's classic story of retribution is one of the great melodramas of the world. Because the sailor Edmund Dantes has honored the dying request of his captain to carry a private letter to Napoleon on Elba, it becomes possible for Fernand, who loves Edmund's wife Mercedes, to have him arrested and imprisoned in the Château d'If. Through years of weary labor, he cuts his way through the wall, to find that instead of attaining freedom, he has only joined the Abbé Faria, who was doing the same thing from the other side. When the Abbé dies, after having given Dantes a chart showing the location of fabulous treasure on the Isle of Monte Cristo, the latter escapes from prison by taking the Abbé's place in his burial sack and causing himself to be cast into the sea. He is rescued and possesses himself of the treasure. Pursuant to his exultant cry "The world is mine!," he disguises himself and returns to France, where he rewards his friends and disposes of his three great enemies, clocking them off as "One!" "Two!" "Three!," and is reunited with Mercedes.

COMMENTARY: In the Spring of 1912, a furrier turned film exhibitor by the name of Adolph Zukor formed the Famous Players Film Company, in association with theatrical producer Daniel Frohman. Despite acquiring the U.S. rights to the French production of *Queen Elizabeth* starring Sarah Bernhardt, and despite the company's announcement that it was to produce only four-reel features starring major Broadway personalities—at a time when virtually all the licensed motion-picture producers were turning out one- and two-reelers—the Famous Players Film Company aroused little interest in the industry. Its competitors were to regret their lack of concern, for Zukor and Famous Players were to grow quickly in importance. In July of 1915, Zukor combined with the Jesse L. Lasky Feature Play Company, and subsequently merged with other producers to become Paramount Pictures Corporation on January 1, 1917. At the time of his death, on July 10, 1976, Zukor was still Chairman Emeritus of Paramount.

For his first production, Zukor chose James O'Neill to repeat his performance in the title role of *The Count of Monte Cristo*, in which O'Neill had appeared on stage more than 4,000 times! To direct, photograph and edit the film, Edwin S. Porter, a good, solid technician but a man who at this stage of his career had little flair for anything new or innovative, was lured away from the Rex Company. In the meantime, the Selig Company hurriedly filmed a three-reel version of *The Count*, featuring Hobart Bosworth under the direction of Colin Campbell, and rather than compete with Selig, Zukor temporarily shelved his production, and commenced on two further features, *The Prisoner of Zenda* with James K. Hackett and *Tess of the D'Urbervilles* with Minnie Maddern Fiske.

When *The Count of Monte Cristo* was finally released, the anonymous critic of *The Moving Picture World* (November 1, 1913) proclaimed that the Dumas story was "now presented in the universal language of the pictures. . . . All the hopes and despairs experienced by the honest sailor lad whom fate torments and tortures, all his dreams and desires and defeats, are typified by Mr. O'Neill's vigorous art until they develop into a semblance of the moving emotions that Dumas intended to weave into the story, and with which he so capably succeeded in surrounding his character." Although O'Neill looks much too old and paunchy for the role, he *does* acquit himself well, particularly in the dueling scene with which the film closes. The painted backdrops are a little too much in evidence, but exterior scenes are not completely forgotten, and, despite its melodramatics, there is still something quite impressive about the scene in which Dantes declares "The world is mine!," with O'Neill standing on a wave-washed rock, silhouetted against the sky.

It is, of course, because of Eugene O'Neill and *Long Day's Journey into Night* that the film holds interest today. It seems highly probable that O'Neill studied his father's performance while working on his masterwork, for the son retained a print of the film all his life. (*A. S.*)

Above: "The tender farewell from Mercedes arouses the jealous hatred of Fernand, a Catalan fisherman secretly in love with Mercedes" (original title). Below: The marriage of Dantes and Mercedes.

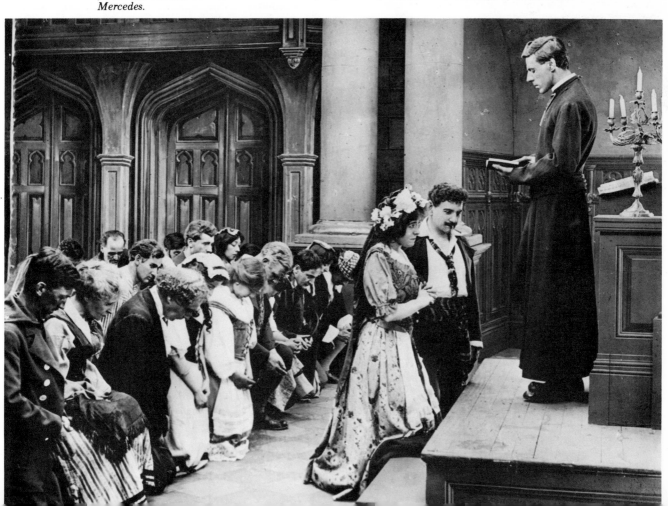

Above: *Dantes tries to tunnel out of his prison cell. (Note the artificiality of the painted set.)* Below: *Dantes, disguised as the Abbe Busoni, exclaims "One!," signifying that one of his enemies has met the fate he deserved.*

TRAFFIC IN SOULS

An Imp production. Released by Universal. World premiere: Joe Weber's Theatre, New York, November 24, 1913. 6 reels.

Director: George Loane Tucker. Screenplay: Walter Macnamara. Film Editor: Jack Cohn.

(There were at least two skits on *Traffic in Souls*: a Joker comedy, *Traffic in Soles*, released March 4, 1914; and *Traffickers in Soles*, released by the Feature Photoplay Company in February of 1914.)

CAST: Jane Gail (*Mary Barton*); Ethel Grandin (*Lorna Barton*); Fred Turner (*Isaac Barton*); Matt Moore (*Larry Burke, Officer 4434*); William Welsh (*William Trubus*); Irene Wallace (*His Daughter*); Mrs. Hudson Lyston (*Mrs. Trubus*); William Cavanaugh (*Bill Bradshaw*); Howard Crampton (*The "Go Between"*); Charles Burbridge (*Inspector Smith*); Arthur Hunter (*The Cadet*); Laura Huntley (*A Country Girl*); William Powers (*The Emigrant Girls' Brother*); Jack Poulton (*R.R. Cadet*); Edward Boring (*Swedish Cadet*); Charles Green (*Butler*); William Calhoun (*Mr. Gesham*); Arthur Stein (*Bobby Gesham*); George Loane Tucker (*Wireless Operator*); Walter Macnamara (*First Cabin Cadet*); Sarah McVicker (*Mrs. Gesham*); Flora Nason (*Swedish Girl*); Vera Hansey (*Her Sister*); Laura McVicker (*Telephone Operator*); Adele Graham (*Madame F. Forster*); Blanche Craig (*Madame McCarrol*).

SYNOPSIS: A young New York girl is shanghaied into a brothel, whereupon her sister and the latter's heroic policeman lover set out to find her. Opportunely, the sister becomes secretary to a wealthy man who is ostensibly the head of the reform league. Through discovering a Dictaphone in his office, she learns that he is "the man higher up" in the vice ring, operating in league with the exploiters in an office on the floor below. She and her lover record the conversations of the criminals, by which means they are brought to justice just in time to wreck the betrothal of the fake reformer's daughter to "the catch of the season." The shock kills his wife, estranges his daughter, and leaves him desolate.

COMMENTARY: Inspired by the Rockefeller White Slavery Report and New York District Attorney Whitman's investigations of vice, *Traffic in Souls* is said to have been made, without Carl Laemmle's authorization, on $5,700 put up by Herbert Brenon, King Baggott, and others. Thirty thousand people saw it during its first week at Joe Weber's Theater, and it was soon playing 28 theaters in greater New York alone and setting off a whole cycle of muckraking films. With George Loane Tucker in England, it had been cut and edited from ten reels to six by Jack Cohn, and the director never saw it on the screen.

In his pioneering history of the American film, *A Million and One Nights*, Terry Ramsaye proclaimed that with *Traffic in Souls* the screen discovered sex. Yet there is absolutely no sexual stimulation in the picture, only indignation against exploiters and grafters. The exposition is almost childishly straightforward, and the whole approach to the problem under consideration now appears amazingly simplistic. The film is drab and sometimes repetitive; there are far too many scenes showing the ghouls dividing the spoils in the office of the go-between, all of which look very much alike. Yet the very absence of "cinema" lends the picture a certain brute force which one cannot but feel even today. It is not all centered upon the main story; much of the first part, semidocumentary in style, shows the white slavers tricking country and immigrant girls into their lairs. The many exteriors of New York City in 1913, with automobiles, streetcars, etc. now looking wonderfully primitive, have added a period interest that *Traffic in Souls* did not have when it was first shown.

For many years, this was considered a "lost" film, but in 1972 an excellent print was found in the Middle West, from which copies were made available to collectors through Blackhawk Films. (*E. W.*)

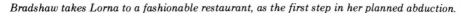

Bradshaw takes Lorna to a fashionable restaurant, as the first step in her planned abduction.

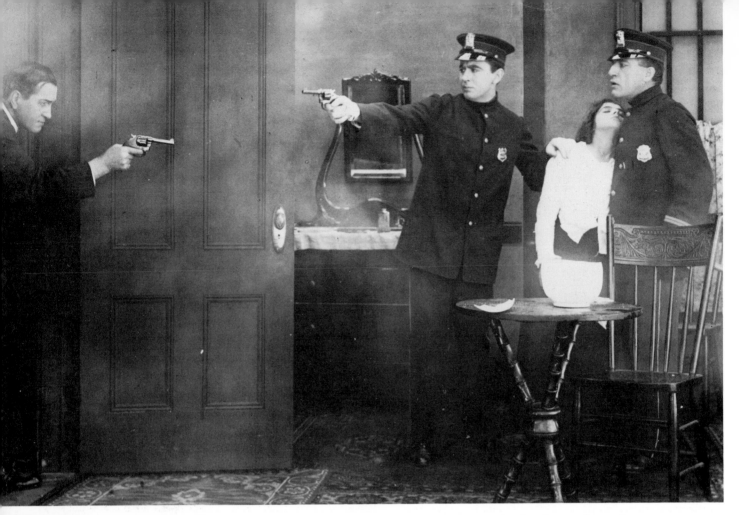

Above: *Officer 4434 shoots it out with the crooks.* Below: *Lorna is restored to her sister as the crooks are rounded up.*

THE SPOILERS

A Selig production. World premiere: Orchestra Hall, Chicago, March 25, 1914. 9 reels.

Producer: Colonel William N. Selig. Director: Colin Campbell. Screenplay: Lanier Bartlett (based on the novel by Rex Beach). Photography: Harry W. Gerstad.

(*The Spoilers* was reissued in 1916 in an expanded 12-reel version, which included footage of Rex Beach. Beach's novel has been filmed four other times: in 1923 by Goldwyn, in 1930 by Paramount, in 1942 by Universal, and in 1955 by Universal-International.)

CAST: William Farnum (*Roy Glennister*); Bessie Eyton (*Helen Chester*); Tom Santschi (*Alex McNamara*); Kathlyn Williams (*Cherry Malotte*); Wheeler Oakman (*Broncho Kid*); Frank M. Clark (*Dextry*); Jack F. Mc-Donald (*Slapjack*).

SYNOPSIS: During the Alaskan Gold Rush, Glennister, part owner of the Midas Mine, finds his claim in dispute. He is suspicious of the motives of McNamara, the gold commissioner. This distrust is shared by Cherry Malotte, owner of the local gambling saloon, who is secretly in love with Glennister, but jealous of his attention toward Helen Chester. Cherry's faro-table dealer, Broncho, is in love with her, and he conspires with McNamara against Glennister to seize the mine and have Glennister accused of murdering the town marshal. Glennister and his supporters try to regain control of the mine and Broncho is killed, but not before revealing the truth. Glennister and McNamara meet in a bloody fist fight, which the former wins. Cherry learns she was mistaken about Glennister's feelings toward Helen, and the two are reconciled.

COMMENTARY: Selig's film of Rex Beach's popular novel of 1906 was the first of some five versions, and it is considered by many to have been the most faithful to the original work. However, the film has a greater claim to fame as one of the American cinema's first major feature-length productions, predating, as it does, *The Birth of a Nation* by some nine or more months. *The Spoilers* was an enormous critical and popular success; *Variety* (April 17, 1914) commented: "To the rabid movie fan—the one who revels in action, excitement and panoramic succession of real life adventures—this picture hands him a wallop." It was chosen to open the new Strand Theatre in New York;

it introduced William Farnum to the screen, and it encouraged the Selig Company to release a series of mammoth productions, including *The Ne'er Do Well* (1915), *The Rosary* (1915), and *The Crisis* (1916).

Those films, as was *The Spoilers*, were directed by Colin Campbell, a long-forgotten technician whose style of direction belonged to the cinema's beginnings. As new film techniques were introduced, Campbell stayed with the stage-oriented, solid, unimaginative directing techniques of the early and pre-teens, and it is interesting to note that his directing style changed not one iota from *The Spoilers* through the 1919 production of *Little Orphan Annie* with Colleen Moore. Colonel Selig and Campbell obviously saw eye to eye as far as filmmaking was concerned, for Campbell stayed with the producer for more than eight years and was entrusted with the handling of all Selig's major dramatic productions.

There is much that is old-fashioned in *The Spoilers*. The dialogue titles feature the unnecessary use of the name of the character who is speaking. Many of the titles are highly melodramatic—for example, at one point a miner announces, "There's never a law of God or man runs north of Fifty-three"—but this is probably a fault carried over from the novel. In fact, Campbell's directing style probably enhances, rather than takes away from, the melodramatics of the original work. The climactic fight sequence between Glennister and McNamara, which opens with the latter's announcement, "I'm going to kill you with my own hands," is extremely well handled, and has an earthy, brutally raw quality to it missing from the later, more sophisticated Hollywood versions, which boasted such protagonists as Gary Cooper versus William Boyd and John Wayne versus Randolph Scott. The reviewer in *The Moving Picture World* was quite carried away by the fight scene, which he thought "so real and so just that we whisper, between breaths, 'Amen.'"

William Farnum and Kathlyn Williams handed in particularly fine performances. To *The Moving Picture World*, Farnum was "force personified," while *Variety* doubted that any actress "could have improved upon the part" played by Kathlyn Williams. Miss Williams, best remembered for her title-role performance in the serial *The Adventures of Kathlyn*, need have played no other part than that of Cherry Malotte in *The Spoilers* to assure herself of screen immortality. (*A. S.*)

Above: Cherry Malotte is introduced to the Alaska of the Gold Rush days. As "The Moving Picture World" (April 3, 1914) commented, "She is the one character among all of them whose soul bears her above her surroundings." Below: Cherry Malotte and Dextry.

Above: *A dramatic moment in the gambling saloon: Glennister, Broncho, and Cherry.* Below: *Glennister confronts McNamara: the climactic fight is about to commence.*

TESS OF THE STORM COUNTRY

A Famous Players production. Released by Paramount on March 30, 1914. 5 reels.

Director, Screenplay (based on the novel by Grace Miller White) and Photography: Edwin S. Porter.

(*Tess of the Storm Country* was remade by Miss Pickford in 1922 under the direction of John S. Robertson. It was subsequently remade in 1932 by Fox, with Janet Gaynor under the direction of Alfred Santell, and in 1960 by 20th Century-Fox, with Diane Baker under the direction of Paul Guilfoyle.)

CAST: Mary Pickford (*Tessibel Skinner*); Harold Lockwood (*Frederick Graves*); Olive Fuller Golden [Mrs. Harry Carey] (*Teola*); David Hartford (*Daddy Skinner*); W. R. Walters (*Elder Graves*); Lorraine Thompson; Louise Dunlap; Richard Garrick; Jack Henry; H. R. Macy; Eugene Walter; H. L. Griffith.

SYNOPSIS: Tessibel Skinner is the daughter of a squatter and poaching fisherman who is unjustly accused of having committed a murder. Elder Graves believes him guilty, but his son Frederick, a theological student, befriends Tess, loves her, and introduces her to an unquestioning religious faith (she "cribs" a Bible from the mission and reads it devoutly). Frederick's friend, Dan Jordan, gets Frederick's sister Teola pregnant and is killed before he can make things right. Tess takes Teola into her hut and keeps the baby there, with the result that she is considered a wanton and even Frederick turns against her. When the baby is at the point of death, Tess marches into the church during a service and herself baptizes it. Teola cries, "Give me my baby!" and the situation is clarified. Both Teola and the baby die, Daddy Skinner is cleared, and Elder Graves changes his mind about the squatter girl.

COMMENTARY: *Tess of the Storm Country* was the fifth film Mary Pickford (1893–1979) made for Famous Players, and its prime significance is that, beyond any other single item, it was responsible for making her the most famous of all screen actresses, a distinction she retained unchallenged throughout the rest of her career. Adolph Zukor's original idea, following his importation of Bernhardt's *Queen Elizabeth*, had been to bring moviegoers "famous players" from the stage. So he did, but most of the big ones were flops. He had no idea at the outset that the little movie actress he also employed was going to be the mainstay of his company. In the first Famous Players film in which she appeared, *In the Bishop's Carriage*, her name had not even preceded the title. Without Mary's brilliant performance, *Tess* would have been just another film. Its director, Edwin S. Porter, had a curious career. He could be startlingly innovative, and he could be purely mechanical. *Tess*, unfortunately, does not show him at his best.

Beside Mary, however, nothing else mattered. People who have never seen her on the screen seem to have the

Frederick instructs Tess in the Bible.

idea that her pictures were saccharine or goody-goody. One would like to prescribe a showing of *Tess of the Storm Country* for them. The girl, to be sure, is good as gold, sometimes even heroic in her goodness, but she is also a spitfire, capable of fighting like a wildcat to protect those she loves. The whole performance is as vigorous as it is nicely shaded.

Miss Pickford's attractive vis-à-vis in this film, Harold Lockwood, soon became a leading male star, but his career was cruelly cut short when he died in the great influenza epidemic of 1918. Miss Pickford's own interest in *Tess* seems sufficiently attested by the fact that, after she had assumed control of her own cinematic destinies, this was the only one of her early successes that she chose to redo. (*E. W.*)

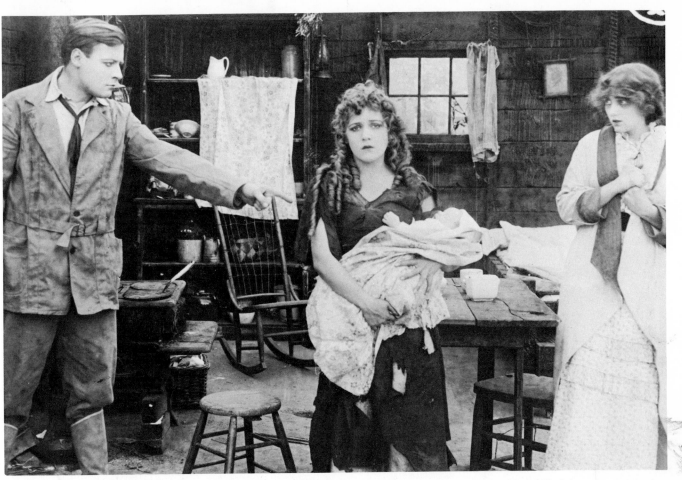

Above: *Frederick thinks Tess the mother of Teola's child.* Below: *Tess stealing milk for Teola's baby. Caught and punished, she says, "I have been whipped. Now can I have the milk?"*

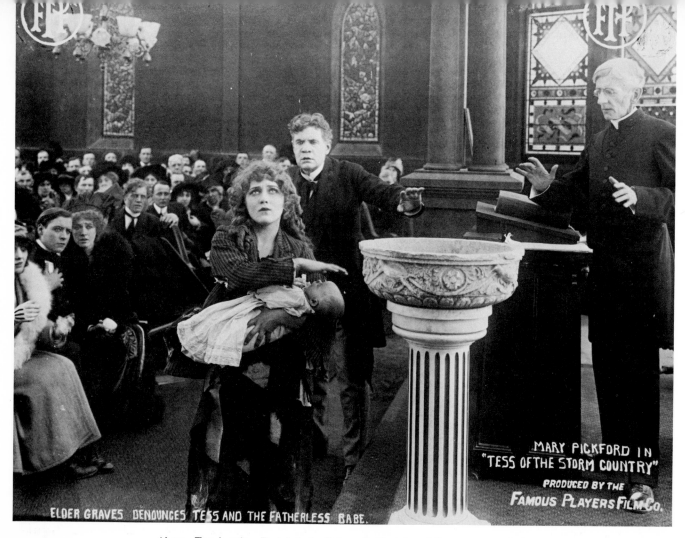

ELDER GRAVES DENOUNCES TESS AND THE FATHERLESS BABE.

MARY PICKFORD IN "TESS OF THE STORM COUNTRY"

PRODUCED BY THE FAMOUS PLAYERS FILM Co.

Above: *Tess baptizes Teola's baby.* Below: *Frederick and Tess are reconciled.*

THE BARGAIN

A New York Motion Picture Corporation production. Released by Paramount Pictures on December 3, 1914. 5 reels.

Producer: Thomas H. Ince. Director: Reginald Barker. Screenplay: William H. Clifford and Thomas H. Ince. Production Manager: William H. Clifford.

CAST: William S. Hart (*Jim Stokes, the Two-Gun Man*); J. Frank Burke (*Bud Walsh, the Sheriff*); J. Barney Sherry (*Phil Brent*); Clara Williams (*Nell Brent, His Daughter*); Joseph J. Dowling (*Rev. Joshua Wilkes*); Roy Laidlaw (*Miner*); Charles Swickard (*Miner*); Charles K. French (*Bartender*); Herschel Mayall (*Gambler*).

SYNOPSIS: After a successful stagecoach robbery, outlaw Jim Stokes is wounded and takes refuge with the prospector Phil Brent and his daughter Nell. She and Jim fall in love and are married, but shortly after the wedding Jim is captured by Sheriff Walsh. The sheriff takes Jim and the stolen money into custody, but is cheated out of the latter in a gambling hall. Jim strikes a bargain with the sheriff that he will win back the money in return for his freedom, which he does, and Jim and Nell head for the Mexican border together.

COMMENTARY: "The West! The Land of Vast Golden Silences Where God Sits Enthroned on the Purple Peaks and Man Stands Face to Face with His Soul." So reads the title introducing *The Bargain*, William S. Hart's first feature-length Western and arguably his best film. *The Bar-* gain is a film superbly directed and edited, and, above all, exquisitely photographed (probably by Joseph August); the beautiful panoramic shots in and around the Grand Canyon are awe-inspiring. One interesting novelty is to introduce each player, in evening dress, at the beginning of the production, and, then, as they bow to the audience, have them become the characters they portray in the film.

The story begins as a typical Western melodrama, but suddenly, in reel four, takes a surprising turn when "the bargain" is struck between the sheriff and Hart. Critical reaction to the film was mixed. *Variety* (November 13, 1914) described it as "one of the best feature-length Westerns ever shown," and compared Hart's performance to the artistic creation of a Frederic Remington painting. However, W. Stephen Bush in *The Moving Picture World* (December 5, 1914) wrote, "*The Bargain* is nothing more than an old-fashioned 'Western.' I cannot truthfully say that it is one inch above the average of such pictures." The reviewer was also disturbed by the moral question raised by "the bargain" and the sheriff's gambling, and noted, "There can be no doubt whatever that a picture of this kind has a bad influence on youthful minds." Obviously the dramatic power of the last title—"No star is lost we once have seen; we always may be what we might have been"—was completely lost on him.

The Bargain must be given credit as the production that transformed William S. Hart the stage actor into William S. Hart the movie star. It set a standard, in terms of both production and moral values, for all his later features. (*A. S.*)

The prospector Phil Brent and his daughter Nell take Jim Stokes to their cabin under the misapprehension that he has been wounded by Indians.

Above: *Stokes declares his love to Nell. (The love of a good woman persuading an outlaw to go straight was a continuing theme in the films of William S. Hart.)* Below: *The sheriff captures Stokes in a gambling saloon, as the gambler looks on. (Both J. Frank Burke and Herschel Mayall were long-time Ince contract players, never star material but always reliable character men.)*

Above: *Stokes confesses his past to Nell. (Clara Williams was a leading lady with Ince for a number of years, also appearing in* THE ITALIAN; *she retired from the screen in 1920.)* Below: *Scenes such as this led Peter Milne in "Motion Picture News" (November 21, 1914) to comment, "The exteriors, photographed in the Arizona canyon, offer a sequence of glorious views in which the rugged wilderness of a virgin country predominates."*

A FOOL THERE WAS

A William Fox production. Released by the Box Office Attraction Company in January, 1915. 6 reels.

Director: Frank Powell. Screenplay: Roy L. McCardell (based on the play by Porter Emerson Browne and the poem by Rudyard Kipling). Photography: Lucien Andriot.

(*A Fool There Was* was remade by Fox in 1922, starring Estelle Taylor and Lewis Stone under the direction of Emmett J. Flynn.)

CAST: Theda Bara (*The Vampire*); Edward Jose (*The Fool* [*Mr. John Schuyler*]); Mabel Fremyear (*The Fool's Wife* [*Mrs. John Schuyler*]); May Allison (*The Wife's Sister*); Runa Hodges (*The Child*); Clifford Bruce (*A Friend*); Victor Benoit (*A Victim of the Vampire*); Frank Powell (*The Doctor*); Minna Gale (*The Doctor's Fiancée*).

SYNOPSIS: "The Fool" is commissioned to go abroad on a mission for his country, but his wife and child are unable to accompany him owing to the illness of the wife's sister. On board ship, "The Fool" becomes infatuated with "The Vampire," who desires him as a plaything. At her bidding, he forgets his diplomatic duties, turns to alcohol and drugs, and deserts his wife and child. "The Fool" becomes a pitiful object. As he crawls to the side of "The Vampire," she orders, "Kiss me, my fool," but as he attempts to reach her he dies. With an inscrutable smile, "The Vampire" scatters rose petals over his body.

COMMENTARY: Acting ability aside, there can be no question that the most outrageous female personality spawned by the film industry in the teens was Theda Bara. Although not the screen's first vamp, it was she who popularized the character and encouraged countless imitators of her style, the best of whom were Louise Glaum and Valeska Suratt. Her first feature, *A Fool There Was,* laughable as it may appear, and undoubtedly is today,

captivated the less sophisticated audiences of 1915. Theda Bara, née Theodosia Goodman of Cincinnati, literally became an overnight sensation, proving perhaps for the first time the value the film industry could, and would, place on publicity, however fraudulent. The film's producer, William Fox, just about founded his company on the success of *A Fool There Was.* Only its director, Frank Powell, a pupil of D. W. Griffith at Biograph, failed to reap any substantial rewards from the film, possibly because even in 1915 it was obvious that the direction had no relevance to the success of the production, and the direction, such as it was, was on a par with the melodramatics of Miss Bara and her fellow players.

Since Julian Johnson had not at that time begun his column of film criticism in *Photoplay,* we must rely for contemporary comments on the trade reviewers, all of whom seemed totally unaware of the silliness of the plot and all of whom were taken in by Miss Bara. Margaret I. MacDonald, in *The Moving Picture World* (January 30, 1915), referred to Theda Bara's "inimitable interpretation," while Peter Milne in *Motion Picture News* (January 23, 1915) thought she played "with great skill." Milne continued, "Aside from the fact that it will do the very young little good, and perhaps harm, to witness the film, it is exceedingly excellent. It will absorb all classes; it is convincingly and powerfully acted; bears the marks of excellent direction, and is photographed well, and little more could be asked."

Viewed today, *A Fool There Was* fascinates with its mediocrity and its totally unbelievable plot. That a generation of moviegoers could have been taken in by its almost self-parodying characterizations is almost impossible to believe. Yet it never fails to hold one's attention. *A Fool There Was* may not have been one of the greatest artistic productions of the teens, but it was certainly one of the most entertaining. (*A. S.*)

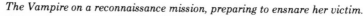

The Vampire on a reconnaissance mission, preparing to ensnare her victim.

Above: *The Vampire gloats while the Fool lies dead at her feet. (Although it was not at all apparent from his work in* A FOOL THERE WAS, *Edward Jose was a prominent stage actor and a former leading man to Sarah Bernhardt.) Below: A publicity shot of Theda Bara for* A FOOL THERE WAS. *(After reviewing the production in 1952, S. J. Perelman was forced to admit, "For all its bathos and musty histrionics,* A FOOL THERE WAS *still retains some mysterious moral sachet.")*

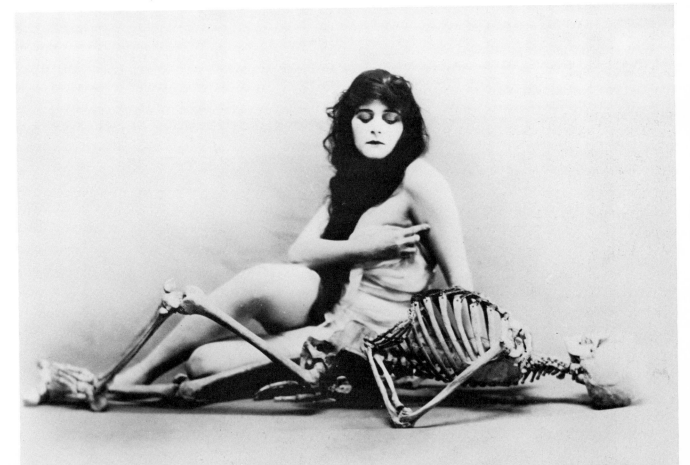

HYPOCRITES

A Bosworth production. World premiere: Longacre Theatre, New York, January 20, 1915. Subsequently released by Paramount, October 19, 1915. 4 reels.

Director and Screenplay: Lois Weber. Associate Director: Phillips Smalley. Photography: Dal Clawson. Art Director: Frank Ormston.

(A film under the same title was released by Cosmofotofilm Company in 1918, directed by George Loane Tucker, and based on the sex drama by Henry Arthur Jones.)

CAST: Courtenay Foote (*Gabriel*); Myrtle Stedman (*A Magdalene*); Margaret Edwards (*The Naked Truth*); Jane Darwell.

SYNOPSIS: Gabriel, an ascetic monk of the early years of Christianity, perfects an image of Truth, but when it is unveiled before the villagers and found to be naked, he is stoned to death. Only a little child and a Magdalene, who loves Gabriel, can look upon truth. A thousand and more years pass, and Gabriel is now pastor to the same people who stoned his former self to death. The villagers are shocked when he denounces hypocrisy, and only the woman who loves him and the Magdalene understand. After his sermon, Gabriel comes across a reproduction of the painting *The Truth*. His spirit, clothed in the form of Gabriel the ascetic monk, leaves his present-day body and, accompanied by Truth and her mirror, sees the real character of the people. The mirror proves them all to be hypocrites.

COMMENTARY: The American silent cinema boasted thirty or more women directors, most of whom were responsible for the production of one or two features and then disappeared from the scene. Only two, Alice Guy Blache and Lois Weber, were of unquestionable talent, and only the latter both directed and scripted her own productions in a career that lasted more than twenty years. It is not easy to select a representative Lois Weber production.

One might choose her best known, *Where Are My Children?* (1916), for its anti-abortion stand, or one might select *The Dumb Girl of Portici* (1916), which featured Anna Pavlova in her only film. But the present choice, *Hypocrites,* typifies Weber's lack of timidity over the controversial nature of her films and demonstrates her total commitment to presenting her point of view on social or political issues.

Hypocrites cannot have been an easy film to make. It is allegorical, and allegories seldom evoke much enthusiasm from studio heads or from film audiences. It used a naked female figure as its central character at a time when any form of even seminudity was unheard of in the American cinema. It attacks the establishment, presenting hypocrisy and corruption in government, business, and the church. As with so many of her productions, Lois Weber demonstrated tremendous courage in taking a stand against that which she believed wrong, just as earlier she had fought anti-Semitism in *The Jew's Christmas* (1913), and later was to attack capital punishment in *The People vs. John Doe* (1916).

There were those who condemned *Hypocrites*—the Ohio Board of Censors banned it, and the Mayor of Boston demanded clothing be painted, frame by frame, onto the Naked Truth—but most people, inside and out of the film industry, found much to admire in the production. To the critic of *Motography* (October 24, 1914), it was the technical aspects which impressed: "Not only double and triple exposures, but even sextuple exposures make the picture remarkable." *Variety's* Sime (November 6, 1914) summed up the reaction of most critics: "There is no other picture like it, there has been no other, and it will attract anywhere, for it is a pretty idyllic pastoral picture of faultless taste. The title, *Hypocrites,* is faithfully carried out for the theme. As a moving picture, in the manner Miss Weber has done this film, it could be truthfully proclaimed as the essence of sweetness in purity, but you will have to see the picture before realizing that. It is quite remarkable from every angle of the picture art." (*A. S.*)

Gabriel: "Ye Cannot Enter."

Above: *The sermons of Gabriel disturb his fellow monks. (The telephone pole is something of an anachronism for a scene set in 900 A.D.)* Below: *Scenes such as this typified Lois Weber's stand against corruption in government and big business.*

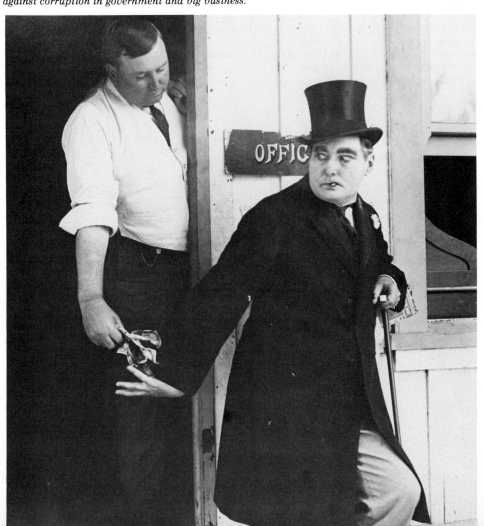

Above: *Lois Weber's view of the American politician, a view it is doubtful she would have changed sixty years later! (The woman is Jane Darwell, an actress best known to filmgoers for her performances as Ma Joad in* THE GRAPES OF WRATH *and the Bird Woman in* MARY POPPINS.) Below: *The hypocrite is represented by the liar and cheat: a dramatic moment illustrating Lois Weber's use of double exposure to emphasize her point.*

THE ITALIAN

A New York Motion Picture Company production. Released by Paramount Pictures, January 7, 1915. 5 reels.

Producer: Thomas H. Ince. Director: Reginald Barker. Screenplay: C. Gardner Sullivan and Thomas H. Ince.

CAST: George Beban (*Beppo Donnetti*); Clara Williams (*Annette Ancello*); J. Frank Burke (*Gallia, Annette's Father*).

SYNOPSIS: Beppo Donnetti, a handsome young gondolier, is in love with Annette Ancello, but her father will not allow their marriage until Beppo is able to provide for his daughter. Hearing of the wonderful opportunities in America, Beppo goes there, and within a year is able to send for Annette. In time a baby is born to them, but is taken seriously ill during an intense heat wave that sweeps over New York. The doctor tells Beppo the baby must have pasteurized milk or die. On his way for the milk, Beppo is robbed by two gangsters. He appeals to Boss Corrigan for help, but is turned down and jailed for five days, during which time the baby dies. When Corrigan's child is taken ill with brain fever and absolute quiet is demanded, Beppo seeks his revenge. He enters Corrigan's house and is about to create a disturbance and precipitate the baby's death when the child places its arm under its chin in a gesture similar to one used by Beppo's child. Moved by compassion, Beppo sneaks away.

COMMENTARY: *The Italian* is one of those films which, quite rightly, have achieved a considerable reputation in recent years, but which, on their initial release, received little if any mention. It was briefly reviewed in *The New York Dramatic Mirror* and *Variety,* but completely ignored by *The Moving Picture World,* the most influential trade paper of the day.

George Beban, the star of the film and its chief raison d'être, had made a speciality of playing Italian characters. On the stage since the age of eight—he was known as "The Boy Baritone of California"—he had won praise for his performance in his own play, *The Sign of the Rose,* which Ince filmed in 1915 as *An Alien,* and which Beban remade in 1922 under the original title.

Thomas Ince signed George Beban to make his screen debut in the late summer of 1914, and assigned Reginald Barker to direct him in an original motion picture with the working title of *The Dago.* The ghetto scenes were shot, in October, on location in Los Angeles and San Francisco. *Reel Life* (November 21, 1914) announced that Beban and a cameraman would journey to Italy to shoot "fifty odd scenes" for *The Italian,* but the nearest the company got to Italy was Venice, California.

The Italian is a grim tale of an Italian immigrant and his wife who see in the United States a land of opportunity, a land of happiness. In reality, it is a land where everything is to work against them: the environment, the authority of the police and those in power, and, above all, the corruption. The misery of life in this country is well illustrated by comparison to the Italian's peaceful existence in his own land. In one touching scene, a subtitle, "Youth, heated by the fires of love and ambition, rushes on to meet the future," introduces Beban and Clara Williams walking happily along the crest of a hill. The next title, "While old age, ever shrinking back, stops to warm itself by the dying embers of the past," shows Williams' father by his fireside, followed by a shot of the young lovers silhouetted on a clifftop, looking out to sea, while the sun sets in the distance. The memory of this scene is ever-present as the tale of hardship and poverty of American ghetto life unfolds.

One interesting aspect of the film's technique is that it opens with George Beban, the actor, reading a book, *The Italian,* by C. Gardner Sullivan and Thomas Ince. (As is commonly known, Ince always put his name on everything to do with his productions, but it is highly unlikely that he contributed anything to the screenplay.) This prologue helps to heighten the effectiveness of Beban's characterization of the poor Italian immigrant, but it also, unfortunately, seems to imply that this is only a story; it could never happen. At the film's close, Beban puts down his book. The curtains close, and the play is over.

The reviewer in *The New York Dramatic Mirror* (December 30, 1914) probably came closest to realizing that *The Italian* was something out of the ordinary. "The production is notable," he wrote. "More than that, one might safely name it as unique among the pictures scheduled on the Paramount programme—a programme confessedly aimed at a more cultivated public than has been reached by that useful trinity, bathos, sentimentality, and melodrama."

George Beban continued to make films until his death in Los Angeles on October 5, 1928, but none of them achieved the reputation of his first production, *The Italian.* (A. S.)

Above: *Annette, Beppo, and Gallia in a happy moment early in* THE ITALIAN. *Below: The Italian brings his new bride to their first home in the new land.*

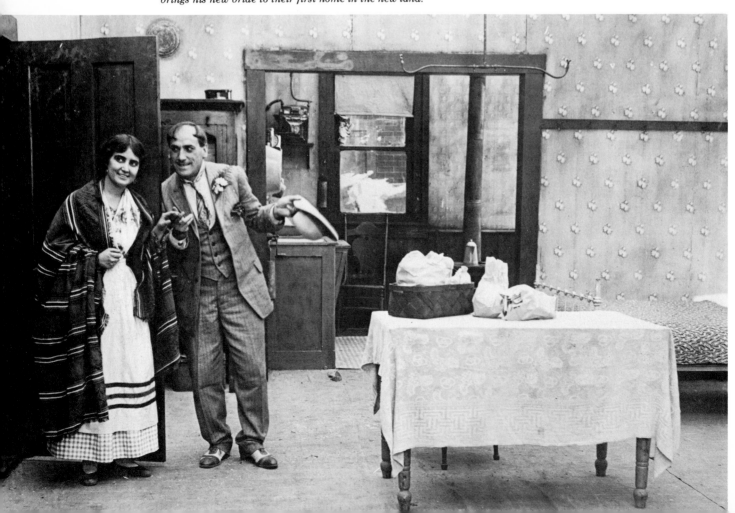

Above: *George Beban as the archetypal Italian. (With regard to Beban's clothing in* THE ITALIAN, *Thomas H. Ince recalled, "One day he caught sight of an immigrant coming ashore at the Battery. George flanked him and in good Italian offered to take over everything on the stranger's back in return for a fair price paid therefor. George secured the complete outfit, including headgear and footgear, for ten dollars, and despite its notorious age and fears for another hard winter, called it a bargain.") Below: The Italian and his wife are introduced to the realities of American life as the doctor informs them that their baby must have pasteurized milk, which they cannot afford, if it is to live.*

25

THE WARRENS OF VIRGINIA

A Jesse L. Lasky Feature Play Company production. Presented by Jesse L. Lasky in association with David Belasco. Released by Paramount Pictures, February 15, 1915. 5 reels.

Producer and Director: Cecil B. DeMille. Screenplay: William C. de Mille (based on his own play). Photography: Alvin Wyckoff.

(*The Warrens of Virginia* was remade by Fox in 1924, starring Martha Mansfield under the direction of Elmer Clifton.)

CAST: Blanche Sweet (*Agatha Warren*); James Neill (*General Warren*); Page Peters (*Arthur Warren*); Mabel Van Buren (*Mrs. Warren*); Marguerite House [Marjorie Daw] (*Betty Warren*); House Peters (*Ned Burton*); Dick La Reno (*General Griffin*); Mrs. Lewis McCord (*Sapho*).

SYNOPSIS: Agatha Warren, the daughter of an aristocratic Southern general, is in love with Ned Burton of New York, but at the outbreak of the Civil War they become estranged and Burton enlists with the Union army. The years pass, and Burton is forced by his superior officers to use his intimacy with the Warren. family to prevent a supply train from reaching the beleaguered Confederate army. He is captured, and Agatha offers him the means of escape, which pride prevents him from accepting. However, just as he is to be shot, Lee surrenders at Appomattox, and the lovers are reunited.

COMMENTARY: Just as Adolph Zukor's Famous Players Company chose Mary Pickford to represent the film star in its company of players, so did Jesse L. Lasky and Cecil B. DeMille select Blanche Sweet, the leading actress with D. W. Griffith's stock company, to be the star of their new company. As a vehicle for the actress, DeMille selected *The Warrens of Virginia* by his brother William, which had been a popular success on stage for a number of years and in which Cecil B. DeMille himself had appeared in a minor role.

Blanche Sweet recalls, "I had a terrible time. So did DeMille. I had never worked for any other director, except one or two things, than Griffith, and here I was with a strange director that I didn't know anything about, and didn't know much about his films—he hadn't made many. His version of the story was that he was terrified of me. He was working with a Griffith player who was supposed to have quite a reputation, and he didn't know much about films himself. And here the two of us sat, staring at each other. Afterwards he said, 'You know you used to give me those hard looks. I thought you were saying this man doesn't know what he's talking about.' I said, 'No, on the contrary, Cecil. I was looking attentively at you, trying to find out what you wanted from me.' We didn't get along. We just didn't spark."

The Warrens of Virginia evoked only mild critical interest; it was perhaps overshadowed by a larger Civil War drama, *The Birth of a Nation,* which opened almost simultaneously. However, *The Warrens* is not without its better points. The battle scenes are as good as anything directed by Griffith, the plot is compact and directed at a steady, intelligent pace, and Miss Sweet, who admittedly is not required to do too much, does what she does well. Blanche, leading man House Peters, and DeMille followed *The Warrens of Virginia* with *The Captive,* a more complex story with a Montenegro background. Of the two, Blanche Sweet prefers *The Captive,* but both illustrate an ability in both star and director which would stand them in good stead in the years ahead. (*A. S.*)

Agatha and General Warren. (W. Stephen Bush in "The Moving Picture World" of February 27, 1915 described the latter's performance as "thoroughly capable and conscientious and effective.")

Above: *The women of the Warren household at work for the Confederate cause: Mrs. Warren, Betty, and Agatha.* Below: *A beautifully composed shot of Arthur and Agatha.*

Above: *Agatha offers to help Union spy Ned Burton escape.* Below: *A dramatic moment at the close of* THE WARRENS OF VIRGINIA: *Ned Burton, Arthur Warren, General Warren, and Agatha. (Note the director's chair in the right foreground!)*

THE BIRTH OF A NATION

An Epoch Producing Corporation production. First screening (as *The Clansman*): Loring Opera House, Riverside, California, January, 1915. Los Angeles premiere (as *The Clansman*): Clune's Auditorium, February 8, 1915. New York premiere (as *The Birth of a Nation*): Liberty Theatre, March 3, 1915. 12 reels.

Producer and Director: D. W. Griffith. Screenplay: D. W. Griffith and Frank E. Woods (based on the novel and play *The Clansman,* by Thomas Dixon). Photography: G. W. Bitzer. Assistant Cameraman: Karl Brown. Film Editor: James Smith. Costumes: Robert Goldstein. Music Score: Joseph Carl Breil and D. W. Griffith. Assistant Director: Thomas E. O'Brien.

(*The Birth of a Nation* was reissued in a shortened version in 1930 with music and sound effects. For this version, D. W. Griffith supervised a prologue, consisting of a conversation between himself and Walter Huston, overheard by three children: Byron Sage, Betsy Heisler, and Dawn O'Day [Anne Shirley]. For the prologue, Karl Struss was the photographer, Bert Sutch assistant director, and Edward Seward head electrician.)

CAST: Lillian Gish (*Elsie Stoneman*); Mae Marsh (*Flora Cameron, the Little Sister*); Henry B. Walthall (*Colonel Ben Cameron, the Little Colonel*); Miriam Cooper (*Margaret Cameron*); Mary Alden (*Lydia Brown, Stoneman's Mulatto Housekeeper*); Ralph Lewis (*The Hon. Austin Stoneman, Leader of the House*); George Siegmann (*Silas Lynch/Leader of Confederate Soliders Who Rescue Piedmont*); Walter Long (*Gus, a Renegade Negro*); Robert Harron (*Tod Stoneman/A Negro Soldier*); Wallace Reid (*Jeff, the Blacksmith*); Joseph Henabery (*Abraham Lincoln*); Elmer Clifton (*Phil Stoneman*); Josephine Crowell (*Mrs. Cameron*); Spottiswoode Aitken (*Dr. Cameron*); George (André) Beranger (*Wade Cameron*); Maxfield Stanley (*Duke Cameron*); Violet Wilky (*Flora as a Child*); Jennie Lee (*The Faithful Mammy/Woman at Abolitionists' Meeting*); Donald Crisp (*General U. S. Grant*); Howard Gaye (*General Robert E. Lee*); Sam De Grasse (*Senator Charles Sumner*); Raoul Walsh (*John Wilkes Booth*); Eugene Pallette (*A Fallen Foe to Whom Ben Cameron Gives Succor*); John McGlynn (*Nelse, an Old-Fashioned Negro*); Ernest Campbell (*Jake, a Black Man Faithful unto Death*); Madame Sul-Te-Wan (*One of the Female Slaves Who Mock Dr. Cameron*); John Ford (*A Clansman*); Elmo Lincoln; Olga Grey; William De Vaull; Tom Wilson; David Butler; Pauline Starke.

SYNOPSIS: The plot is built around the friendship between the younger members of a Southern family, the Camerons, and the children of the fanatical Northern leader Austin Stoneman (modeled on the historical Thaddeus Stevens). The oldest Cameron son, Ben, later the "Little Colonel," falls in love with Elsie Stoneman, and the older Stoneman son loves Margaret Cameron, but North-South differences postpone the marriages until the end. Elsie's younger brother and the two younger Cameron sons are killed in the war, and the "Little Colonel" is seriously wounded in a charge against a Northern trench commanded by Phil Stoneman. While in hospital in Washington, Ben is condemned to death on a false charge, but Elsie takes his mother to Lincoln, who pardons him.

The assassination of Lincoln puts the radical Republicans under Stoneman in charge of Reconstruction. They are committed to the policy of "putting the white South under the heel of the black South." Stoneman's henchman in Cameron territory is an ambitious, conscienceless mulatto, Silas Lynch, who becomes lieutenant-governor of the state and who lusts after Elsie Stoneman. Ben Cameron becomes involved in organizing the Ku Klux Klan, which is used, among other things, to avenge the death of Flora Cameron, the "Little Sister," who dies when she jumps from a high rock to save herself from rape by Gus, a renegade Negro. Toward the end, all the principals are brought together in the Camerons' hometown of Piedmont, where Elsie is being held by Lynch while the others are besieged in a cabin out of town. All persons are rescued by the Klansmen, and general reconciliation ensues on both a personal and ideational level.

COMMENTARY: A little more than one hundred years ago, on a small farm in Kentucky, David Wark Griffith was born. There is every reason for ever to celebrate that event. If Griffith had not come along, perhaps we would have the movies as we know them today, or perhaps we would not. For it was D. W. Griffith who took a cheap form of entertainment, which had been in existence a mere dozen years when he began directing, and created an art form. Griffith laid the foundation stone of the art of the cinema. Others have come along since and built upon that foundation, but they have added little. There was little that could be added; Griffith had done it all before.

Much has been written of Griffith's having invented the close-up, editing, etc., while he was at Biograph. He did not invent those techniques—they had been in use long before he entered films—but he did perfect their use. He did not invent film editing, but he did create the art of film editing. He was not the first director to shoot a close-up, but he was the first director to shoot a close-up for dramatic effect. These and other artistic techniques Griffith perfected during the five years he was with the Biograph Company; the Biograph shorts, one might say, were his training ground.

And when the training was complete, from the polishing of the director's skills at Biograph, came *The Birth of a Nation*, one of the greatest productions, and certainly the most important, in the history of American film. It revolutionized the cinema far more than the so-called milestones, such as *Gone with the Wind, Citizen Kane,* and *Star Wars,* since. The intervening years cannot and will not dim the acting performances of Lillian Gish and others, the spine-tingling shots of the Klan riding to the rescue, the sighing of the "mooning" sentry, the realism and heroism of the battle scenes, the heartrending death of Mae Marsh as the Little Sister, or the earthy quality to the fight scene involving Wallace Reid, so eye-catching that it was to make of its protagonist a star. Yet, despite its brilliance, in recent years the film has come to be known, not because of the masterpiece it is, but because of the assertion of premeditated and deliberate racism.

In 1919 a critic wrote of D. W. Griffith, "He paints the lily. He refines pure gold. He adds another hue to the rainbow. He works in an understanding way for those who understand." All those who love cinema will both understand and admire *The Birth of a Nation* for what it is—the ultimate masterpiece of the American silent screen—not for what recent detractors have tried to make of it. (*A. S.*)

Above: *Old Plantation Days: little Flora, Ben, Margaret, and Phil.* Below: *One of the spectacular battle scenes.*

Above: *The Little Colonel leads the charge against the Union soldiers.* Below: *The Little Sister terrified by the renegade Gus.*

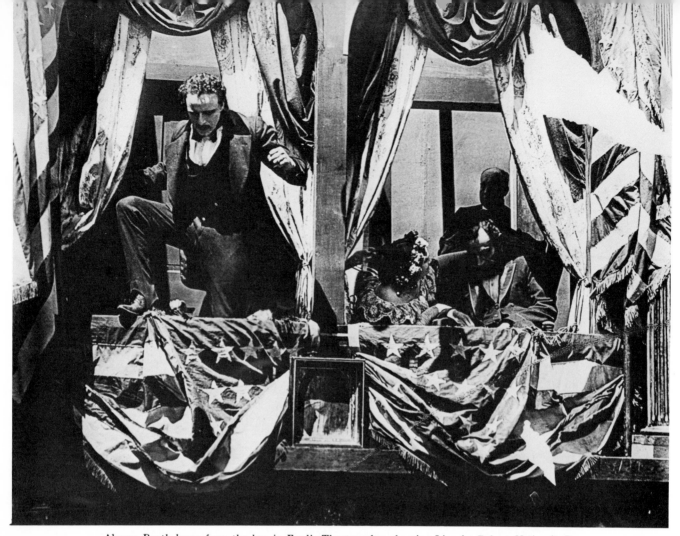

Above: *Booth leaps from the box in Ford's Theatre after shooting Lincoln.* Below: *Voting in Reconstruction Days.*

Above: *Elsie Stoneman about to be menaced by Silas Lynch.* Below: *The Ku Klux Klan on the road.*

CARMEN

A Jesse L. Lasky Feature Play Company production. Released by Paramount Pictures, November 1, 1915. 5 reels.

Producer and Director: Cecil B. DeMille. Screenplay: William C. de Mille (based on the story by Prosper Mérimée). Photography: Alvin Wyckoff. Music Score: Melville Ellis.

(*Carmen* has been the subject of at least 14 motion pictures.)

CAST: Geraldine Farrar (*Carmen*); Wallace Reid (*Don José*); Pedro de Cordoba (*Escamillo*); Horace B. Carpenter (*Pastia*); Billy Elmer (*Morales*); Jeanie Macpherson (*Gypsy Girl*); Anita King (*Gypsy Girl*).

SYNOPSIS: Carmen, an amoral but vital and beautiful Gypsy girl, in league with smugglers, fascinates the officer Don José and deflects him from his duty long enough to permit her confederates to bring their goods into the city. After a fight with another girl in the tobacco factory where both are employed, Carmen is taken into custody by Don José, but when he is drawn into mortal combat over her with Morales, she escapes to the mountains, and Don José deserts and follows. Carmen soon leaves him for the toreador Escamillo. Don José follows her to Seville, and when she spurns him, he stabs her outside the bullring in the very moment of Escamillo's triumph.

COMMENTARY: When, through Morris Gest, Jesse L. Lasky bagged America's most famous prima donna, Geraldine Farrar, for the still comparatively humble art of the movies, he gave the screen a prestige shot in the arm which recalled that administered by Sarah Bernhardt when she appeared in *Queen Elizabeth,* which Adolph Zukor had imported into this country in 1912 as the first Famous Players film. Even without her voice, Miss Farrar proved a great attraction, and for five years she devoted her summers to making films.

She traveled to Hollywood in a private car, with her parents and friends, and was paid the highest salary the company had yet offered anybody, plus all kinds of special treatment and fringe benefits. When she arrived, the mayor of Los Angeles was on hand to greet her, and when *Carmen* had been completed, it was shown first, with great fanfare, on October 1, 1915, within the sacred precincts of Symphony Hall, in the star's own Boston.

She made three films her first summer in Hollywood— *Maria Rose, Carmen,* and *Temptation.* Though *Carmen* was released first, they were made in that order, to allow her to become accustomed to the new medium before shooting the piece de résistance. Pedro de Cordoba was in all three films. Wallace Reid, beginning the important phase of his short, brilliant, and ultimately tragic career, was in *Carmen* and *Maria Rose.* There are excellent accounts of Miss Farrar's adventures in Hollywood in both her autobiography, *Such Sweet Compulsion* (Greystone Press, 1938), and DeMille's *Autobiography* (Prentice-Hall, 1959).

Out of copyright considerations, *Carmen* followed the Mérimée story, not the libretto of the opera; there was therefore no Micaëla. But probably few moviegoers noticed the difference. Miss Farrar was naturally allowed more action on the screen than in the Metropolitan Opera House, and her characterization was therefore somewhat more earthy than on the stage, where she remained closer to the French operatic tradition. *Carmen* was an excellent film, a sensational success in its time, which has aged very gracefully, especially if one can see it in the beautifully tinted original exhibition print owned by George Eastman House. (*E. W.*)

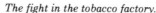

The fight in the tobacco factory.

Above: *Carmen after the fight in the tobacco factory.* Below: *Carmen with Don José at the hole in the wall that accommodates the smugglers.*

Above: *Carmen with Don José and Morales.* Below: *Carmen looks on unconcernedly while Don José fights Morales.*

THE COWARD

A Kay-Bee production. Released by Triangle, November 14, 1915. 6 reels.

Producer: Thomas H. Ince. Director: Reginald Barker. Screenplay: C. Gardner Sullivan.

CAST: Frank Keenan (*Colonel Jefferson Beverly Winslow*); Charles Ray (*Frank Winslow*); Gertrude Claire (*Mrs. Winslow*); Margaret Gibson (*Amy*); Nick Cogley (*A Negro Servant*); Charles K. French (*Confederate Commander*).

SYNOPSIS: Colonel Winslow is a fire-eating Southern militarist of the old school, and when the Civil War comes, he drives his sensitive son Frank to the recruiting office in their Virginia village under threat of death. Assigned to picket duty, Frank runs away in terror the first night and takes refuge in the family house, where he is comforted by his mother and his "mammy," but when his humiliated father learns what has occurred, he himself enlists as "Private Winslow" to perform the duty his son had shirked. When Union officers take possession of the house, Frank, now hiding in the attic, overhears their plans to surprise the Confederates. He knocks down a Union sentry, steals his coat, and rides off to give warning. His father, on sentry duty, not recognizing his son in his disguise, shoots him, but he survives and gives the warning that enables the Confederates to survive the Union attack. The film ends with the reconciliation of father and son.

COMMENTARY: The basic idea of *The Coward* is the same as that of Griffith's one-reel Civil War Biograph, *The Battle* (1911), the story of a coward who redeems himself in a crisis, though in the Griffith film the hero (Charles West) was taunted by his sweetheart (Blanche Sweet) rather than by his father. The almost insane glorification of the military virtues in *The Coward* stands in the sharpest possible contrast to the pacifism of the nearly contemporaneous *Civilization* and raises interesting questions as to what Ince really believed about war, if anything.

The Coward is generally remembered as having established Charles Ray, who proceeded to a number of years of great success as the screen's leading male ingénue or "barefoot boy." An actor of great charm, if limited equipment, he did not manage his career wisely, and after he had nearly bankrupted himself with an inept production of *The Courtship of Miles Standish* in 1923, the great days were over. He died, still comparatively young, in 1943.

It was the stage actor Frank Keenan who was starred in *The Coward,* however. It was his first film and the Kay-Bee offering on the second Triangle program at the Knickerbocker Theatre in New York and elsewhere (Griffith's Fine Arts entry was *Old Heidelberg,* with Dorothy Gish and Wallace Reid). *The Moving Picture World* was undisturbed by Keenan's outrageous "mugging," but Julian Johnson in *Photoplay* found him "registering" by winding up his intensity "as laboriously as an ancient grandfather's clock" and thought that he still had "some screen mechanics unlearned." Meanwhile, Ray was an able challenger for top honors. "Not since William Elliott's remarkable but hardly appreciated study of a weak boy in *A Grand Army Man* have I seen so carefully developed, so sincere a depiction, as young Ray's." (*E. W.*)

Colonel Winslow threatens his son, who is reluctant to fight.

Above: *The fugitive is comforted by his mother.* Below: *Mother and son.* (*Despite his establishing himself as a star with his Civil War role in* THE COWARD, *Charles Ray went on to portray bucolic youths with far less pressing problems than the young hero of this film.*)

THE CHEAT

A Jesse L. Lasky Feature Play Company production. Released by Paramount Pictures, December 12, 1915. 5 reels.

Producer and Director: Cecil B. DeMille. Screenplay: Hector Turnbull. Photography: Alvin Wyckoff. Art Director: Wilfred Buckland.

(*The Cheat* was remade twice by Paramount: in 1923 with Pola Negri and Charles De Roche, and in 1931 with Tallulah Bankhead and Irving Pichel.)

CAST: Fannie Ward (*Edith Hardy*); Jack Dean (*Dick Hardy*); Sessue Hayakawa (*Tori*); James Neill (*Jones*); Utake Abe (*Tori's Valet*); Dana Ong (*District Attorney*); Hazel Childers (*Mrs. Reynolds*).

SYNOPSIS: Socialite Edith Hardy gambles on the stock exchange using charity funds which she is holding. She loses the money and, in desperation, borrows ten thousand dollars from Tori, a wealthy Oriental, who seeks her affection. By chance, Edith's husband makes a killing on Wall Street, and gives her ten thousand dollars to spend as she wishes. She seeks in vain to return Tori's money, and he, after denouncing her as a cheat, brands her with a symbol signifying she is his property. In pain, Edith shoots him, but her husband arrives on the scene and accepts responsibility for the crime. Tori recovers from the wound, and at the husband's trial, Edith Hardy confesses the truth and displays the brand on her naked shoulder. A furious courtroom mob tries to lynch Tori, and Edith and her husband are reunited.

COMMENTARY: *The Cheat,* a sex and sadism thriller, daring for 1915, though never grossly handled, is the only film I know from which both a play and an opera (Camille Erlanger's *Forfaiture,* Paris, 1921) were later adapted. Though the New York *Times* called it "sensational trash," both Julian Johnson in *Photoplay* and W. Stephen Bush in *The Moving Picture World* were ecstatic, Bush declaring that "features like this put the whole industry under obligations to the Lasky company." In England too *The Bioscope* lauded the film to the skies: "As a work of art, *The Cheat* has the hard and glittering brilliance of a diamond, as compared with the soft, opalescent beauty of, say, a Mary Pickford film."

Fannie Ward's principal claim to fame is that she was always young and fair. Nobody knows how old she was when she died in 1952, but she is generally believed to have been in her forties when she made this her first film, and she looked twenty years younger. She was a small woman with enormous eyes and a hard mouth. Well cast as the frivolous socialite, she turned in a vivid if highly melodramatic performance. But everybody else in the picture is melodramatic too. Though *Variety* thought Sessue Hayakawa ought to have been starred and the *Times* commended his technique to Miss Ward's study, even he sneers and grimaces frightfully; he was still to develop the subtlety he was later to manifest in a starring career

Edith learns that her husband has made a killing in the stock market and that therefore she did not need to obligate herself to Tori.

considerably more important than hers. (I regret that I cannot see Marcel L'Herbier's 1937 film *Forfaiture,* in which he replayed his original role.)

DeMille introduces his three principals in set poses, formally, ending with "Fannie Ward as Edith Hardy," who thereupon advances smiling, in her absurd clothes, to greet the unseen audience. Thereafter the development is smooth and relatively unpretentious, though the lighting effects with which the director evidently took special pains and which were much praised at the time, seem less impressive now (they might well look better in an original exhibition print), and the famous courtroom scene ends in confusion worse confounded.

The most shocking thing about *The Cheat* today is its naked appeal to race prejudice. Bush, who speaks of "the beastliness of the Oriental nature" in connection with Tori, quotes approvingly from "one of the men who sat behind me in the Strand Theatre" and who wished he could be in the mob that tried to lynch him at the close, and even Johnson praised the picture as "a melodrama so rational, so full of incisive character touches, *racial truths* [my italics] and dazzling contrasts. . . ." When *The Cheat* was reissued in 1918, however, when Japan was our ally, Tori was transmogrified into a Burmese. How much more convenient it would have been if he had had a German face! (*E. W.*)

Above: *Edith with Tori and her husband. (Jack Dean was Fannie Ward's husband in real life.)*
Below: *Edith begs Tori not to telephone her husband with news of her indebtedness to him.*

Above: *Edith shoots Tori after he has branded her.* Below: *Edith Hardy saves her husband by baring her branded shoulder in court.*

PEGGY

A Kay-Bee production. Released by Triangle, February 20, 1916. 7 reels.

Producer and Director: Thomas H. Ince. Screenplay: C. Gardner Sullivan. Photography: Bobby Newman. Music Score: Victor Schertzinger.

CAST: Billie Burke (*Peggy Cameron*); William H. Thompson (*Andrew Cameron*); Charles Ray (*Colin Cameron*); Gertrude Claire (*Mrs. Cameron*); William Desmond (*Rev. Donald Bruce*); Claire DuBrey (*Maid*); Nona Thomas (*Jane McLeod*); Truly Shattuck (*Mrs. Van Allyn*).

SYNOPSIS: Peggy Cameron, a well-to-do, uninhibited, and apparently frivolous American girl, is summoned by her uncle and guardian to his home in a small village near Glasgow. She first scandalizes her pious relatives by arriving in a motor car which she has driven recklessly on the Sabbath, and continues her course by other aspects of unconventional and, in their eyes, unwomanly behavior. But she wins the hearts of the children by telling them enchanting fairy stories. One of her escapades results in curing the village drunkard; later she discovers that the young man responsible for the condition that has subjected the weaver's lass Janet to church discipline is her guardian's own son. By the time this situation has been righted, Peggy has become so much a part of the life of the village that when she plans to return to America, it is the minister himself who gives her reason to stay.

COMMENTARY: Aside from directing an occasional scene, such as one of the romantic moments in Blanche Sweet's *Anna Christie*, Thomas H. Ince ceased to direct any of his productions after 1912, with one exception. His name, as director, would appear on a film's credits and in publicity, through 1916, despite the task having been undertaken by Reginald Barker, Raymond West, and others; but it was Ince and not one of his contract directors who undertook the handling of Billie Burke in her feature film debut, *Peggy*.

Signing Billie Burke was quite a coup for Ince. She was one of the most popular stage actresses of her day—her later appearances in sound films such as *A Bill of Divorcement* and *The Wizard of Oz* hardly do justice to her comedic charms—having experienced considerable success in Arthur Wing Pinero's *The Mind the Paint Girl* and Somerset Maugham's *The Land of Promise*. Ince did everything he could to make her stay at Inceville, his Pacific Palisades studios, as pleasant as possible; he built a new film stage, complete with piano, on ground level, only 200 feet from the Oceanfront road, so that Miss Burke might avoid having to climb the wooden steps traversed by the other Ince players from William S. Hart down. And one actress at the studio recalls that the producer had a private toilet—the only one on the lot—specially installed for his star.

He was wise to show such consideration for Billie Burke, for she proved to be the best thing about *Peggy*. Critics found the story unconvincing and the direction lacking in

Billie Burke as Peggy, "a fountain of natural energy and seemingly exhaustless vigor," according to Louis Reeves Harrison in "The Moving Picture World" (January 22, 1916).

imagination. However, typical of the critical reaction to Miss Burke was that of Julian Johnson in *Photoplay* (April, 1916): "No pretty wanderer into the camera's field ever photographed more exquisitely than Billie Burke. The whimsical little twitches of her lips, the elfin glimpses of her eyes, the cascades of her laughter have been faithfully written down sixteen times a second. No star this season— she is truly entitled to the stellar name, no matter how carelessly the planets are batted about by the press-agents—has twinkled out of such a surrounding constellation. No more lavish inanimate investiture has ever fortified an animate representation. . . . The best thing this picture did was its introduction of a superlative screen comedienne. In one picture Billie Burke takes her place beside anyone you might name for sheer silversheet ability." (A. S.)

Above: *Scenes such as this added a touch of J. M. Barrie whimsy to* PEGGY. *They were introduced by way of having the star recount fairy tales to the Scottish children. Below: A scene from the interpolated fairy story, in which Billie Burke's girlish qualities are seen to advantage.*

Above: *A still illustrating Billie Burke's tomboyish quality; she is about to repair her car much to her dour uncle's dismay.* Below: *Rev. Mr. Bruce, Andrew Cameron, Peggy, Colin Cameron, and others. Stern uncle Andrew relents and allows his son to marry the weaver's daughter in the dramatic climax to* PEGGY.

HELL'S HINGES

A Kay-Bee production. Released by Triangle, March 5, 1916. 5 reels.

Producer: Thomas H. Ince. Directors: Charles Swickard and William S. Hart. Screenplay: C. Gardner Sullivan. Photography: Joseph August. Music Score: Victor Schertzinger.

CAST: William S. Hart (*Blaze Tracey*); Clara Williams (*Faith Henley*); Jack Standing (*Rev. Robert Henley*); Alfred Hollingsworth (*Silk Miller*); Robert McKim (*A Clergyman*); J. Frank Burke (*Zeb Taylor*); Louise Glaum (*Dolly*); John Gilbert; Jean Hersholt.

SYNOPSIS: To the tough Western town of Hell's Hinges, dominated by the saloon and gambling-house keeper Silk Miller, comes the Reverend Robert Henley and his devoted sister Faith. Silk's myrmidons break up the first service, but the respectables find an unexpected ally in Blaze Tracey, who finds himself so captivated and condemned by the purity and friendliness he discerns in Faith that he accepts her God along with her. Silk plans revenge by inviting Henley to his place to hold a service for the dance-hall girls, where Dolly gets him roaring drunk and destroys his self-respect. While Blaze is away to get an organ for the church, the building is burned down and Henley killed. Upon his return, Blaze invades the saloon with two guns firing. Silk is killed and the place set on fire. The conflagration spreads to the rest of the town, and Blaze and Faith depart to seek a better future beyond the mountains.

COMMENTARY: "It is an intensified *Virginian*," said *Photoplay* of *Hell's Hinges*, "perhaps without *The Virginian's* finesse, but with much more than its power. . . . In a frenzy of magnificent action, in suspense which rolls upon itself like a cloud of war-gas, in climaxes which rattled upon each other like the blows of a young prizefighter upon the body of an older antagonist, comes this picture's flaming finish. No, this is not psychologic drama, nor even heart-vivisection. It is simply Western melodrama with a charge of new high-explosive."

That about says it. One may object that no town could exist in such a state of abandoned frenzy as Hell's Hinges, even long enough to be burned down. One may question both the instantaneousness of the minister's fall (weakling though he has always been) and likewise of Blaze Tracey's redemption. One may find the exposition and the development of the action about as subtle as Alfred Hollingsworth's incredible eye-rolling as the villain. But the smashing fury of the climax still holds the interest, and the action shots toward the end have been directed and edited with masterly vigor. And then, besides, there is William S. Hart.

It was G. M. Anderson, pseudonym of Max Aronson, the "ay" of Essanay, who established the Western hero on the screen as Broncho Billy. His achievement was not inconsiderable, and his rugged honesty would be more widely appreciated than it is if more of his many one-reelers of 1910 ff. were still available for inspection. But it was Hart, who lived from 1865 to 1946 and was in pictures from 1914 to 1925, who gave the character its classical embodiment.

As documents, George Mitchell has placed Hart's films beside the paintings of Charles M. Russell and Frederic Remington. Not many film stars have placed great mythopoeic images on the screen; among these, how many besides Hart have created a figure of monolithic grandeur? Of course there were a great many things he could not do; by sophisticated drawing-room standards, he was even capable, at times, of absurdity. But to stop with that is to be a nitpicker. (*E. W.*)

Faith Henley awakens Blaze Tracey's better nature.

Above: *Blaze in Miller's saloon, the central attraction of Hell's Hinges, "a gun-fighting, man-killing devil's den of iniquity."* Below: *Blaze and Faith: "One that is evil, looking for the first time upon that which is good."*

Above: *The Reverend Robert Henley, now debauched and disillusioned, in the mob which prepares to burn the church.* Below: *Blaze comforts Faith beside her brother's body.* (HELL'S HINGES *was filmed in less than two months at a cost of $32,000.*)

CIVILIZATION

A Thomas H. Ince production. World premiere: Criterion Theatre, New York, June 2, 1916. Subsequently released on a states-rights basis. 10 reels.

Producer: Thomas H. Ince. Associate Producer: J. Parker Read, Jr. Directors: Raymond B. West and Reginald Barker. Screenplay: C. Gardner Sullivan. Photography: Irvin Willat, Dal Clawson, and others. Film Editor: Le Roy Stone.

(*Civilization* was reissued in 1931 with a musical score and sound effects.)

CAST: Herschel Mayall (*The King of Wredpryd*); Lola May (*Queen Eugenie*); Howard Hickman (*Count Ferdinand*); Enid Markey (*Katheryn Haldemann*); George Fisher (*The Christ*); J. Frank Burke (*Luther Rolf, the Peace Advocate*); Charles K. French (*The Prime Minister*); J. Barney Sherry (*The Blacksmith*); Jerome Storm (*His Son*); Ethel Ullman (*His Daughter*); Kate Bruce (*A Mother*); Lillian Read (*A Young Child*); Alice Terry; Claire DuBrey.

SYNOPSIS: The King of Wredpryd embarks upon a war of conquest, placing his hope of success upon the inventor Count Ferdinand. But Ferdinand's sweetheart, Katheryn Haldemann, is one of the leading spirits in a women's peace movement, and she converts her lover to the cause. Ferdinand, in charge of a submarine, refuses to sink a passenger liner carrying contraband; there is a mutiny and the submarine is destroyed. During the inventor's subsequent delirium in illness, he encounters the Spirit of Christ and visits hell. Regaining his health, he boldly opposes the war and is condemned to death. Christ takes possession of the King's body and leads him out to see war's devastation, whereupon he experiences a change of heart and the conflict ends.

COMMENTARY: Ideationally, Ince's most ambitious film was a reply to J. Stuart Blackton's militaristic *The Battle Cry of Peace* (1915), which was based upon Hudson Maxim's book *Defenseless America*. Cinematically, it was an attempt to create a super-spectacle in the Griffith manner.

Its allegorical aspects and its religious coloring are very close to Griffith, and some of the crowd effects are worthy of *Intolerance*. Unfortunately they fail to create a comparable effect, not being really integrated into a story almost as silly as the name of the kingdom in which it is supposed to take place. The characters too are not sufficiently realized to interest the spectator very much or appeal very deeply to his sympathies.

The real importance of *Civilization* today is as an historical document. World War I was fought on the screen as well as on the battlefield, and most of the films, especially after America entered the conflict, were on the pro-war side—the best of them, Griffith's *Hearts of the World*, somewhat reluctantly so, as if made against its producer's convictions. At their worst, the pro-war forces descended to such obscene imbecilities as *To Hell with the Kaiser* and *The Kaiser, the Beast of Berlin*. *Civilization* and Herbert Brenon's *War Brides* (which is considered elsewhere in these pages) were the principal, perhaps the only real, entries on the pacifist side. Legend indeed credits the Ince opus with having contributed importantly to Wilson's reelection in 1916 because he had "kept us out of war." On November 25, 1916, *The Moving Picture World* reported that during the campaign Ince had been received at Shadow Lawn "and congratulated . . . on having produced such a splendid film in the form of a message to Humanity. . . . A very large number of prints of *Civilization* with the Presidential endorsement and Mr. Wilson's portrait was [*sic*] shown in various parts of the country during the closing days of the contest." Let the gods of irony make what they will out of the fact that, after America had entered the war six months later, the picture was "rearranged with new titles and inserts of the American flag, etc., as well as President Wilson's great message to Congress." (*E. W.*)

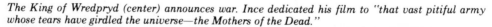

The King of Wredpryd (center) announces war. Ince dedicated his film to "that vast pitiful army whose tears have girdled the universe—the Mothers of the Dead."

Above: *Howard Hickman as Count Ferdinand.* Below: *Count Ferdinand in charge of the submarine.*

The only surviving stills showing soldiers or battle scenes give little indication of the scope of the war sequences or help one appreciate "Variety's" comment (June 9, 1916) that "all told CIVILIZATION ranks with the world's greatest cinema productions."

50

INTOLERANCE

A Wark Producing Corporation production. First screening: Loring Opera House, Riverside, California, August 6, 1916. New York premiere: Liberty Theatre, September 5, 1916. 14 reels.

Producer, Director and Screenplay: D. W. Griffith. Photography: G. W. Bitzer. Assistant Cameraman: Karl Brown. Music: D. W. Griffith and Joseph Carl Breil. Film Editors: James and Rose Smith. In Charge of Set Construction: Frank (Huck) Wortman. Property Master: Ralph DeLacey. Assistant Directors: Arthur Berthelon, Allan Dwan, Erich von Stroheim, W. Christy Cabanne, Tod Browning, Jack Conway, George Nicholls, Lloyd Ingraham, and W. S. Van Dyke.

CAST:

Of All Ages
Lillian Gish (*The Woman Who Rocks the Cradle*).

The Modern Story
Mae Marsh (*The Dear One*); Fred Turner (*Her Father*); Robert Harron (*The Boy*); Sam De Grasse (*Arthur Jenkins*); Vera Lewis (*Mary T. Jenkins*); Mary Alden, Pearl Elmore, Lucille Brown, Luray Huntley, and Mrs. Arthur Mackley (*The Uplifters*); Miriam Cooper (*The Friendless One*); Walter Long (*The Musketeer of the Slums*); Tully Marshall (*A Friend of the Musketeer*); Tom Wilson (*The Kindly Policeman*); Ralph Lewis (*The Governor*); Lloyd Ingraham (*The Judge*); Barney Bernard (*Attorney for the Boy*); Rev. A. W. McClure (*Father Farley*); Max Davidson (*The Kindly Neighbor*); Monte Blue (*A Striker*); Marguerite Marsh (*A Guest at the Ball*); Jennie Lee (*A Woman at Dance of Jenkins' Employees*); Tod Browning (*Owner of the Racing Car*); Edward Dillon (*The Chief Detective*); Clyde Hopkins (*Jenkins' Secretary*); William Brown (*The Warden*); Alberta Lee (*The Wife of the Kindly Neighbor*); George Siegmann (*Judge at Hearing on the Dear One's Baby*).

The Judaean Story
Howard Gaye (*The Christ*); Lillian Langdon (*Mary, the Mother*); Olga Grey (*Mary Magdalene*); Gunther von Ritzau and Erich von Stroheim (*Pharisees*); Bessie Love (*The Bride of Cana*); George Walsh (*The Bridegroom*).

The French Story
Margery Wilson (*Brown Eyes*); Eugene Pallette (*Prosper Latour*); Spottiswoode Aitken (*Brown Eyes's Father*); Ruth Handforth (*Brown Eyes's Mother*); A. D. Sears (*The Mercenary*); Frank Bennett (*Charles IX*); Maxfield Stanley (*Monsieur La France, Duc d'Anjou*); Josephine Crowell (*Catherine de Médicis*); Georgia Pearce [Constance Talmadge] (*Marguerite de Valois*); W. E. Lawrence (*Henry of Navarre*); Joseph Henabery (*Admiral Coligny*); Morris Levy (*Duc de Guise*); Howard Gaye (*Cardinal Lorraine*); Louis Romaine (*A Catholic Priest*).

The Babylonian Story
Constance Talmadge (*The Mountain Girl*); Elmer Clifton (*The Rhapsode*); Alfred Paget (*Belshazzar*); Seena Owen (*Attarea, the Princess Beloved*); Carl Stockdale (*King Nabonidus*); Tully Marshall (*High Priest of Bel*); George Siegmann (*Cyrus the Persian*); Elmo Lincoln (*The Mighty Man of Valor*); George Fawcett (*A Babylonian Judge*); Kate Bruce (*A Babylonian Mother*); Loyola O'Connor (*Attarea's Slave*); James Curley (*The Charioteer of Cyrus*);

Howard Scott (*A Babylonian Dandy*); Alma Rubens, Ruth Darling, Margaret Mooney, and Carol Dempster (*Girls of the Marriage Market*); Mildred Harris and Pauline Starke (*Favorites of the Harem*); Winifred Westover (*The Favorite of Egibi*); Grace Wilson (*The First Dancer of Tammuz*); Lotta Clifton (*The Second Dancer of Tammuz*); Ah Singh (*The First Priest of Nergel*); Ranji Singh (*The Second Priest of Nergel*); Ed Burns (*The Charioteer of the Priest of Bel*); James Burns (*The Second Charioteer of the Priest of Bel*); Martin Landry (*Auctioneer*); Wallace Reid (*A Boy Killed in the Fighting*); Charles Eagle Eye (*Barbarian Chieftain*); William Dark Cloud (*Ethiopian Chieftain*); Charles Van Cortlandt (*Gobyras, Lieutenant of Cyrus*); Jack Cosgrove (*Chief Eunuch*).

Epilogue
Francis Carpenter and Virginia Lee Corbin (*The Children*).

Extras in *Intolerance*, not otherwise listed, included Sir Herbert Beerbohm Tree, Douglas Fairbanks, Owen Moore, Frank Campeau, and David Butler.

SYNOPSIS: *Intolerance* develops the theme of man's inhumanity to man and "love's struggle through the ages" in four interwoven stories, centering respectively about the fall of Babylon to Cyrus the Persian in 538 B.C.; the life of Christ; the Massacre of St. Bartholomew in Paris, August, 1572; and a modern story, set in an American mill town and city slum. The Christ story presents only three episodes from His life, and the French story, also comparatively undeveloped, focuses on a Huguenot family and the older daughter's betrothed, all of whom perish in the massacre. Most of the footage goes into the Babylonian and modern stories. Shots of a woman rocking a cradle are used to mark transitions and emphasize continuity.

The fall of Babylon is presented as a calamity for civilization, and Belshazzar and his father as champions of religious toleration against the fanatical priest of Bel, who betrays the city to Cyrus. Belshazzar is adored by the Mountain Girl and himself loves the Princess Attarea, who dies with him when the city falls. The Mountain Girl too dies fighting for him, after an heroic ride to bring him news of Cyrus' approach, but he is convinced too late to close the gates.

The principals in the modern story are driven to the city after a mill strike, occasioned by a cut in wages to finance the Jenkins "charities." The father of the "Dear One" dies; the "Boy," unable to find employment, becomes a petty thief; the "Friendless One," hungry and penniless, is seduced by a "Musketeer of the Slums," the boss of the "Boy's" gang. Under the influence of the "Dear One," whom he marries, the "Boy" goes straight, but the "Musketeer," in revenge, "frames" him, and he is sent to prison. The "Uplifters," financed by Jenkins, take the "Dear One's" baby away from her, judging her no fit mother. Ultimately the "Friendless One" shoots the "Musketeer," but the "Boy" is condemned to death for the murder and saved only when he is standing on the gallows, after a race between an automobile and a locomotive to record the "Friendless One's" confession and secure a pardon from the Governor.

COMMENTARY: There can be little question that *In-*

tolerance is the greatest motion picture of the silent era, if not the greatest motion picture in the history of the cinema. Nothing can compare to it in terms of innovative techniques and visual splendor, and few films can boast a more human and moving story, a story so magnificent in its emotionalism that it does not pale, but rather blossoms, beside the scenes of historical pageantry and the like. The story to which I refer is, of course, the Modern Story, played by Mae Marsh and Robert Harron with performances that touch the heart to a degree that has seldom been equaled. Mighty as is the Babylonian story, religiously accurate as is the Judaean sequence, touching as is the French episode, it is the compassion of the Modern Story that holds the film together, that constantly holds the attention of the audience and that provides the most biting criticism of social injustice and intolerance.

Intolerance has been foolishly described as Griffith's act of contrition for *The Birth of a Nation*, which is nonsense, for he had already commenced work on *Intolerance* before the latter's release and before the first wave of unfair criticism. Rather *Intolerance* is a continuance of Griffith's basic theme of tolerance and brotherly love, a theme that can be traced back to his Biograph productions, that made its mark with *The Birth*, reached its zenith with *Intolerance*, and that the director continued to preach through *Broken Blossoms*, *Way Down East*, and *Orphans of the Storm*.

That one man could have conceived of a production such as *Intolerance* is staggering; that one man could have brought the conception to fruition despite tremendous odds, both technical and financial, seems impossible. Despite its flaws—and it would be wrong of anyone to suggest that *Intolerance* or any great work of art for that matter is perfect—it has stood the test of time and will continue to stand the test of time as a monument to a man who first understood that film was not just an industry but also an art, a man with an unswerving faith in human decency and a firm understanding of human frailty, a self-taught man with a message, and a man who was the first to present a film audience not with what it wanted to see and what it wanted to know, but what it should experience and should be aware of. *Intolerance* is *the* milestone of the silent film and D. W. Griffith *the* milestone director. (*A. S.*)

Left: *The meeting of the Boy and the Dear One.* Right: *The boy saved from the gallows.*

Above: *Lillian Gish as the Woman Who Rocks the Cradle, linking the four stories and illustrating the continuity of life.* Below: *The Christ on the way to Calvary.*

Above: *Catherine de Médicis and her allies persuading the King to order the Massacre of St. Bartholomew's.* Below: *The massacre begins.*

Above: *In Babylon before the attack.* Below: *Cyrus attacks Babylon.*

A DAUGHTER OF THE GODS

A William Fox production. New York premiere: Lyric Theatre, October 17, 1916. 10 reels.

Supervising Director: J. Gordon Edwards. Director and Screenplay: Herbert Brenon. Titles: Hettie Gray Baker. Photography: A. Barlatier, Roy Hunt, A. Culp, W. Marshall, C. Richards, Marcel Le Picard, and E. Warren. Art Director: John D. Braddon. Modeller: Herbert Messmore. Master of Properties: Joseph Allan Turner. Costumes: Irene Lee. Chief Electrician: F. Sullivan. Technical Director: George Fitch.

CAST: Annette Kellerman (*Anitia, a Daughter of the Gods*); William E. Shay (*Prince Omar*); Hal de Forest (*The Sultan*); Mlle. Marcelle (*Cleone, Prince Omar's Handmaiden*); Edward Boring (*An Arab Sheik*); Violet Horner (*Zarrah, His Daughter, the Sultan's Favorite*); Milly Liston (*Zarrah's Mother*); Walter James (*The Chief Eunuch of the Sultan's Palace*); Stuart Holmes (*A Moorish Merchant*); Walter McCollough (*Chief of the Sultan's Guard*); Ricca Allen (*The Witch of Badness*); Henrietta Gilbert (*The Fairy of Goodness*); Katherine Lee (*Nydia*); Jane Lee (*Little Prince Omar, the Sultan's Son*); Mark Price (*A Slave Dealer*); Louise Rial (*His Wife*).

SYNOPSIS: A childhood fantasy, which begins with a young girl releasing her caged canary. It plays with a sparrow, which is subsequently eaten by a dog, and then, in its loneliness, flies out over the sea until it falls. Meanwhile a royal child, experiencing the same feelings as the canary, sends its spirit flying over "the ocean of eternity." This complex fantasy was described as follows in the original program for *A Daughter of the Gods:* "The Prologue: The plaything of a little child escapes its earthly prison. And thereby hangs a tale of many years ago. Act One: The Land of a Mighty Sultan, and a record of many strange happenings there. A Fairy Prince and Princess Meet. Act Two: Wherein we all become children again and fight for a beautiful Princess. The Land of the Great Beyond. The Fairy Prince and Princess meet again, never to be parted."

COMMENTARY: Herbert Brenon and Annette Kellerman first worked together on *Neptune's Daughter*, the star's first feature-length production, shot on location in Bermuda for release by Universal in 1914. It was considered one of the most spectacular productions of its day, and when Brenon went to work for William Fox in 1915, it was perhaps natural that he should suggest embarking on an even more sumptuous production, to be shot again in the British West Indies, but this time on Jamaica. The director spent nine months working on *A Daughter of the Gods*, building, among other things, a Spanish fort, a complete Moorish city and a special hundred-foot tower for Annette Kellerman's spectacular dive into the ocean. When Fox, by all accounts the most frugal of film producers, learned of the cost and time involved in making the film, he fired Brenon and removed his name from the credits, a move that led directors from then on to insist in their contracts that a producer could not arbitrarily expunge their names from a film.

William Fox had little reason to complain, for *A Daughter of the Gods* was to be a tremendous critical and box-office success. Annette Kellerman's nude (except for a preponderance of artificial hair) diving scenes created a sensation. Here was a fairy tale without precedents in the

Annette Kellerman as Anitia, a daughter of the gods. (As Julian Johnson commented in "Photoplay," "Occasionally Miss Kellerman cavorts like an H₂O primadonna, getting quite out of the play to sing an optic cadenza of splash.")

history of the cinema; armies of gnomes and elves marched across the screen, mermaids frolicked in the surf, and a Sultan's palace, more magnificent than anything pictured in *The Thousand and One Nights*, glistened in the sun. For sheer spectacle, *A Daughter of the Gods* outclassed *Cabiria*, *The Last Days of Pompeii*, and *The Birth of a Nation*. "Here is a stunning photoplay which is a marvel of its kind, and the proclaimer of its author-maker as a master-director of first order," commented Julian Johnson in *Photoplay* (August, 1916). "We are beguiled, we are bewitched, we lose the perception of time and we get back to the naked realities of life like one who is waking from a lovely dream," wrote W. Stephen Bush in *The Moving Picture World* (November 4, 1916). Brenon's foreword to the film entreated, "Let us return to our mother's knee tonight, with the fairies and witches and gnomes and elves, and be as little children to enter a heaven of rich enjoyment." And for the almost three hours in which *A Daughter of the Gods* was on the screen, audiences were happy to obey.

The film's popularity continued long after its initial release. When Fox reissued the production in 1920, it was advertised as "the screen marvel that will never know a yesteryear"—a tribute that only a genuine classic of the screen could hope to achieve. (*A. S.*)

Above: *Annette Kellerman contributed little acting talent to* A DAUGHTER OF THE GODS, *but rather indulged in a considerable amount of posing.* Below: *Sumptuous sets such as this led Julian Johnson to comment, "Architecturally* A DAUGHTER OF THE GODS *is another Troy."*

ROMEO AND JULIET

A Metro production. New York premiere: Broadway Theatre, October 19, 1916. 8 reels.

Director: John Noble. Associate Directors: Edward Elsner and Rudolph De Cordova. Screenplay: John Arthur, Rudolph De Cordova, and John Noble (based on the play by William Shakespeare). Photography: R. J. Berquist.

(*Romeo and Juliet* is one of the most popular of Shakespearian plays with moviemakers, having been filmed more than twenty times, the most famous versions being those by George Cukor in 1936, Renato Castellani in 1954, and Franco Zeffirelli in 1968.)

CAST: Francis X. Bushman (*Romeo*); Beverly Bayne (*Juliet*); Robert Cummings (*Friar Laurence*); Adella Barker (*The Nurse*); Joseph Dailey (*Peter*); W. Lawson Butt (*Tybalt*); Edmund Elton (*Lord Capulet*); Helen Dunbar (*Lady Capulet*); Eric Hudson (*Lord Montague*); Genevieve Reynolds (*Lady Montague*); Horace Vinton (*Escalus*); Olaf Skavlan (*Benvolio*); Fritz Leiber (*Mercutio*); William H. Burton (*The Bishop of Verona*); Harry Sothern (*Abram*); Ethel Mantell (*Rosaline*); Leonard Grover (*An Old Man of the Capulet Family*); Leonard Grover, Jr. (*Uncle to Capulet*); Barry Macollum and Norman Macdonald (*Servants*); Marie Booth (*A Court Lady*); Alexandre J. Herbert (*Friar John*); Violet Hall-Caine (*A Member of the Capulet Family*); Venie Atherton (*A Court Lady*); Barry Maxwell (*Apothecary*); John Davidson (*Paris*); John Burke; Lewis Sealy; Edwyn Eaton; E. P. Sullivan; Morgan Thorpe; Alexander Loftus; Robert Vivian; Edwin Boring; Ben Higgins; Charles A. Smily; A. P. Kaye; Joseph Robison; Jack Blake.

SYNOPSIS: The screen version of *Romeo and Juliet* follows the action of the Shakespeare play except that Rosaline, the girl of whom Romeo is enamored before meeting Juliet, is shown, not merely talked about. The Montagues and Capulets are at deadly enmity; when Romeo and Juliet fall in love, they are secretly married by Friar Laurence. But Juliet's cousin Tybalt draws Romeo, against his will, into a street fray in which both Romeo's friend Mercutio and Tybalt himself are slain. Romeo is exiled and leaves Verona after one secret night with Juliet. The Capulets, ignorant of the marriage, now thrust Paris upon Juliet as a husband, and Friar Laurence gives her a potion to simulate death. But his letter to Romeo miscarries. Believing his love dead, Romeo comes to the vault to take his leave of her; there he is accosted by Paris, whom he slays before poisoning himself. Juliet kills herself with his dagger, and the tragic death of the lovers at last reconciles their houses.

COMMENTARY: As Robert Hamilton Ball has indicated in his scholarly and unimpeachable text *Shakespeare on Silent Film* (Theatre Arts Books, 1968), William Shakespeare is the author who appealed most to the American silent filmmaker, an attraction perhaps helped by the playwright's works all being in the public domain. Some of the best and the earliest literary adaptations were the Vitagraph Company's productions of *Romeo and Juliet* (1908), *Othello* (1908), *Macbeth* (1908), *Richard III* (1908), *A Midsummer Night's Dream* (1909), *Twelfth Night* (1909), and *King Lear* (1909). In the teens, the Fine Arts Company produced *Macbeth* (1915), Universal filmed *The Merchant of Venice* (1914), and, in 1916, two companies filmed *Romeo and Juliet*.

In the early Spring of 1916, Metro commenced production on a screen adaptation of *Romeo and Juliet*, featuring the cinema's most popular romantic duo, Francis X. Bushman and Beverly Bayne, fresh from acting triumphs with the Essanay Company. The casting was perfect from a box-office viewpoint, but somewhat questionable in terms of historic accuracy, for Bushman looked, and was, far too old to play Romeo. No sooner had Metro's version been announced than William Fox embarked on a second production of *Romeo and Juliet*, with his biggest contract star, Theda Bara, portraying Juliet, a casting even more box-office oriented and far more dubious than Metro's.

Of the two productions, it was the Metro one which, quite rightly, received the critical acclaim, and which must be regarded as the most auspicious American film version of a Shakespearian play in the teens. It boasted sumptuous sets, sincere and intelligent acting from its principals, who were required to speak Shakespeare's dialogue, and it also claimed a number of Shakespearian acting names from the stage. These were not *the* great stage actors, but rather distant relatives—not Edwin Booth but Marie Booth, not E. H. Sothern but Harry Sothern. There were also a Mantell and a Loftus, proving that as far as Metro was concerned there was quite a lot in a name.

Julian Johnson in *Photoplay* (January, 1917), reviewing Metro's "sunpainting of the great Veronese love tragedy," pointed out that while Metro's was the superior of the two versions of *Romeo and Juliet*, it was the Theda Bara film that the public would flock to see, and that would thus introduce the masses to the glories of Shakespeare. "Metro's *Romeo and Juliet* seeks as its goal the artistic perpetuation of a great story. It is just that," he wrote. "Fox's *Romeo and Juliet* aims to be a thrilling entertainment. It is."

Perhaps the final critical judgment should be left to George Blaisdell in *The Moving Picture World* (November 4, 1916): "Metro has done the screen a distinct service. Not only has it lavished its best on the adaptation of a great tragedy; not only has it brought it out in all its strength and beauty, its glamor and romance, for the education as well as entertainment of countless thousands who heretofore may have had slight acquaintance with it or concern about it. It has demonstrated that Shakespeare dead three hundred years penned in his youth lines that stamp him the greatest title builder in the world of today." (A. S.)

Above: *Romeo and Juliet. (Francis X. Bushman and Beverly Bayne were once the screen's most popular romantic couple.)* Below: *The Nurse and Juliet.*

Above: *Friar Laurence, Romeo, and Juliet.* Below: *"For never was a story of more woe, than this of Juliet and her Romeo."* *(Even in death, Bushman assures that his classic profile is seen to advantage.)*

WAR BRIDES

Joan. (Nazimova strikes a classic pose for her role.)

A Selznick production. Premiere: Broadway Theatre, New York, November 12, 1916. 8 reels.

Director and Screenplay (based on the stage play by Marion Craig Wentworth): Herbert Brenon. Photography: J. Roy Hunt.

CAST: Nazimova (*Joan*); Charles Hutchinson (*George*); Charles Bryant (*Franz*); William Bailey (*Eric*); Richard Barthelmess (*Arno*); Nila Mac (*Their Sister*); Gertrude Berkeley (*Their Mother*); Alexander K. Shannon (*The King*); Robert Whitworth (*Lieutenant Hoffman*); Ned Burton (*Captain Bragg*); Theodora Warfield (*Minna*); Charles Chailles (*A Financier*).

SYNOPSIS: The heroine of *War Brides* demonstrated her capacity for leadership in a strike before the beginning of the war which has taken her husband to his death in battle. Strongly tempted to end her own life, she lives for the sake of her unborn child, and when the king decrees that young, unmarried women must mate with soldiers leaving for the front, she organizes the women to protest against this plan to produce more cannon fodder. She is condemned to death but imprisoned instead when found to be pregnant. Escaping from jail, she leads the women, with their babies, to protest the war before the king, when he passes through the village.

COMMENTARY: In a 1936 *Theatre Arts* interview, Alla Nazimova described her basic approach to acting: "The actor should not play a part. Like the Aeolian harps that were hung in the trees to be played only by the breeze, the actor should be an instrument played upon by the character he depicts." It was a philosophical approach to acting which Madame Nazimova transferred from her great Ibsen stage roles in *Hedda Gabler*, *A Doll's House* (which she filmed in 1922), and *The Master Builder* to her screen appearances in *The Red Lantern* (1919), *Camille* (1921), *Salome* (1923), and the film that marked her first appearance before the motion-picture camera, *War Brides*.

Nazimova had starred in Marion Craig Wentworth's one-act play on the vaudeville stage, and created something of a sensation, dramatically preaching pacifism at a time when much of Europe was embroiled in a war that within a year was also to engage the United States. The screen rights to *War Brides* were acquired by Herbert Brenon, and after seeing and liking *A Daughter of the Gods*, and being assured of a cash payment of a thousand dollars a day, Nazimova agreed to star in the production. It was not only Nazimova's screen debut, but also introduced Richard Barthelmess in his first major role, which was ultimately to lead to a contract with D. W. Griffith and two decades of stardom.

War Brides opened to favorable reviews from all critics, with the only negative comment concerning the slow development of the plot, a problem occasioned by the producers having to "pad out" a fifteen-minute play into eighty-odd minutes of screen time. "There is a wealth of painstaking detail, good acting, splendid trench and pastoral scenes," commented Hazel Simpson Naylor in *Motion Picture Magazine* (April, 1917). "Beyond the shadow of a doubt it is the best thing that Herbert Brenon has ever done," wrote Peter Milne in *Motion Picture News* (November 25, 1916). "His direction here is excellent. His straight scenes are effectively arranged, the action is centered—easy to follow. He has utilized close-ups to advantage—employed subtitles and excerpts from the play effectively. The standard of production is above criticism. Many of the exteriors are mindful of great paintings. The lighting is superb and the photography excellent."

In *The Moving Picture World* of December 2, 1916, Edward Weitzel published a lengthy and detailed criticism of the production, particularly invaluable as the film is no longer extant: "Its scenes are laid in a hypothetical country, and its characters have the idealism and mysticism of the Russian peasant whose mind has been awakened. Realism and symbolism go hand in hand through the play, and only a very strong story could triumph over so many repeats of scene. The Joan of Nazimova, in her fierce resentment of the war bride decree and her out-spoken determination that she and her sex in general shall rear no more children to become food for cannon, belongs to the band of social firebrands that have been exiled, imprisoned or executed in the cause of Nihilism. For a brief space, it resolves itself into an unmistakable piece of Woman's Suffrage propaganda. . . . To Nazimova and her associates belongs the credit of a fine artistic achievement in the acting of the play—a masterly control of the emotions and their expression by means of the silent drama. The Russian actress' one flaw is in giving too freely of her inward fire. A woman of her intellectual and histrionic breadth need but sit in judgment upon her own work to correct the faults incidental to a first attempt."

Despite the critical praise, Nazimova's performance did not persuade producer Lewis Selznick to star her in another feature, and it was left to Metro to sign her to a long-term contract and fully exploit the actress' talents. (*A. S.*)

Above: *Franz bids his wife Joan farewell as he leaves for the war from which he will never return. (Nazimova and Bryant, though never legally married, lived together for many years as man and wife.)* Below: *Minna, Joan, and the mother. (Of Gertrude Berkeley's performance, Edward Weitzel in "The Moving Picture World" of December 2, 1916 wrote, "an example of screen acting that for beauty, truth and quiet force has never been excelled.")*

OLIVER TWIST

A Jesse L. Lasky Feature Play Company production. Released by Paramount, December 11, 1916. 5 reels.

Director and Screenplay (based on the novel by Charles Dickens): James Young. Photography: Harold Rosson. Art Director: Wilfred Buckland. Costumes based on the original illustrations by George Cruikshank.

(Charles Dickens' novel has been filmed many times, the best-known versions being those in 1922 with Jackie Coogan, in 1933 with Dickie Moore, and in 1948 with John Howard Davies, and the 1968 musical version with Mark Lester.)

CAST: Marie Doro (*Oliver Twist*); Hobart Bosworth (*Bill Sikes*); Tully Marshall (*Fagin*); Raymond Hatton (*The Artful Dodger*); James Neill (*Mr. Brownlow*); Elsie Jane Wilson (*Nancy*); Harry Rattenbury (*Mr. Bumble*); Carl Stockdale (*Monks*); W. S. Van Dyke (*Charles Dickens*); Edythe Chapman (*Mrs. Brownlow*).

SYNOPSIS: This production of *Oliver Twist*, the story of the workhouse boy who falls into the hands of the infamous Fagin to be trained in thievery, follows the plot of Dickens' novel with reasonable fidelity. Among the highlights are Oliver's asking for more gruel, his falling in with Fagin and his gang, his befriending by Mr. Brownlow, his betrayal of the thieves by giving the alarm when they force him to enter a house they intend to rob, the murder of Nancy by Bill Sikes after she has taken Oliver's part, Sikes's death while trying to avoid capture, and the final establishment of Oliver's identity.

COMMENTARY: To present an actress of such exquisite delicacy as Marie Doro (1882–1956) in a male role may, upon first consideration, seem altogether bad casting;

actually it was an inspiration. Dickens did not dramatize essentially boyish qualities in Oliver; the character is rather an avatar or apotheosis of abused innocence, and Miss Doro, an established Broadway actress who had already done the part on the stage and who accounted it her favorite role, was just right for it. Her film career began with Lasky and lasted several years; she later made films in England, France, and Italy, but retired from the theater altogether in 1922.

Though the novel *Oliver Twist* is presented less "scenically" than *A Tale of Two Cities*, it is full of "strong" situations which have always registered with equal effectiveness on stage and screen. The filmmakers gave Miss Doro an exceptionally strong supporting cast. Tully Marshall was quite as fearsome a Fagin as Lon Chaney was to be in the Jackie Coogan production or as Nat Goodwin, who did the role on the stage with Miss Doro, was in the 1912 five-reeler in which he starred. Hobart Bosworth, who as a veteran screen actor embraced nobility and brutality with equal ease, and pretty much everything in between, milked the role of Bill Sikes for all it was worth, and Raymond Hatton, an actor of power who never had any difficulty in making himself look like a little worm when his role required it, was perfect as The Artful Dodger. Aside from his objection to seeing Miss Doro on the screen at the close *in propria persona*, placed over against herself as Oliver (a device that recalls Sarah Bernhardt's taking a bow at the end of *Queen Elizabeth*), it is no wonder that the reviewer in *The Moving Picture World* could find no fault with this film save that it was too short. And indeed the wealth of material in the Dickens novel might have been better accommodated in seven or eight reels than in the five allotted. (*E. W.*)

Oliver asks for more.

Above: *Oliver at the Brownlows'*. Below: *Oliver, Fagin, Sikes, and The Artful Dodger.*

Above: *Fagin threatens Oliver.* Below: *Nancy overhears Fagin and Sikes plotting mischief. (Elsie Jane Wilson was later to become a director at Universal.)*

JOAN THE WOMAN

A Cecil B. DeMille production, produced at the Lasky Studios and exploited by the Cardinal Film Corporation. Premiere: 44th Street Theatre, New York, December 25, 1916. 10 reels.

Producer and Director: Cecil B. DeMille. Screenplay: Jeanie Macpherson. Photography: Alvin Wyckoff. Art Director: Wilfred Buckland. Music Score: William Furst. Assistant Director: Cullen B. Tate. Stuntman: Leo Nomis.

CAST: Geraldine Farrar (*Joan of Arc*); Raymond Hatton (*The Dauphin, later Charles VII of France*); Hobart Bosworth (*General La Hire*); Theodore Roberts (*Cauchon*); Wallace Reid (*Eric Trent*); Charles Clary (*La Tremouille*); James Neill (*Laxart*); Tully Marshall (*L'Oiseleur, the Mad Monk*); Lawrence Peyton (*Gaspard*); Horace B. Carpenter (*Jacques d'Arc*); Cleo Ridgely (*The King's Favorite*); Lillian Leighton (*Isambeau*); Marjorie Daw (*Katherine, Joan's Sister*); Stephen Gray (*Pierre, Joan's Brother*); Ernest Joy (*Robert de Beaudricourt*); John Oaker (*Jean de Metz*); Hugo B. Koch (*The Duke of Burgundy*); William Conklin (*John of Luxembourg*); Walter Long (*The Executioner*); Billy Elmer (*Guy Townes*); Emilius Jorgensen (*Michael*); Ramon Novarro (*A Starving Peasant*).

SYNOPSIS: *Joan the Woman* follows the historical outline of the life of Joan of Arc, but it has a Prologue and Epilogue concerned with an unhistorical English soldier, Eric Trent, who, after a fashion, loves Joan and betrays her, and who, reincarnated, atones by dying for France in World War I. This, obviously, was designed to increase the film's appeal to wartime audiences, and DeMille afterwards rightly regarded it as a mistake.

COMMENTARY: Geraldine Farrar's second summer in Hollywood, 1916, was entirely devoted to the filming of DeMille's first great historical spectacle, rather foolishly entitled *Joan the Woman* because Jeanie Macpherson thought this stressed the humanity of an historical character. It was a phenomenally hot summer, and Miss Farrar's associates never ceased to wonder at her exhaustless energy and unfailing good humor. There was real danger involved, not only in the scene showing Joan's burning at the stake, but in the battle scenes, especially for a lady notoriously afraid of horses, who had to be lifted upon her steed when wearing her armor and who was then virtually helpless in her perilous eminence. In one sequence, Miss Farrar was obliged to stand immersed in a water-filled trench, while DeMille trembled lest her singer's throat be infected with laryngitis. It was not. His was.

Joan of Arc was Miss Farrar's very favorite heroine ("I spent as much thought and energy in making her live again—if only on the shadow stage—the blessed Maid of

Joan with her banner.

Orleans, as upon any of my opera creations"), and though *Joan the Woman* was not quite the box-office "smash" that *Carmen* had been, it was always her favorite film. The sensitiveness of her own performance matched its athleticism, and the only reasonable criticism that can be entered is that she was 34 by the time she came to it and therefore a little mature for the role. If she could have had it ten years earlier, it would have been perfect.

She received excellent support from a brilliant cast, and DeMille achieved some startling, truly imaginative photographic effects, some of which involved the use of color. If *Joan the Woman* was not so great a film as either *Intolerance* or *The Birth of a Nation*, it was still the only American picture of its time that could reasonably compare with them, as contemporary critics realized. (*E. W.*)

Above: *Joan in Domrémy.* Below: *Geraldine Farrar with Raymond Hatton as the Dauphin.*

Above: *Joan in prison, with Wallace Reid as Eric Trent.* Below: *Death at Rouen.*

SNOW WHITE

A Famous Players Film Company production. Released by Paramount, December 25, 1916. 6 reels.

Producer: Adolph Zukor. Director: J. Searle Dawley. Based on the fairy tale by the Grimm Brothers. Photography: H. Lyman Broening.

(*Snow White* has been filmed at least six times, the most famous version being that by Walt Disney in 1937.)

CAST: Marguerite Clark (*Snow White*); Creighton Hale (*Prince Florimond*); Dorothy G. Cumming (*Queen Brangomar*); Lionel Braham (*Berthold, the Huntsman*); Alice Washburn (*Hex, the Witch*); Jimmy Rosen, Herbert Rice, Billy Platt, Major Doyle, Major Criqui, Irwin Emmer, and Addie Frank (*The Dwarfs*).

SYNOPSIS: After Princess Snow White's mother dies, the ugly lady-in-waiting Mary Jane aspires to the throne. A witch makes her beautiful and changes her name to Brangomar, after which the king falls in love with her and marries her. When he is killed while hunting, Brangomar becomes ruler and turns Snow White into a Cinderella. Prince Florimond falls in love with her upon meeting her accidentally, without knowing she is the princess he has come to woo, whereupon the jealous Brangomar orders Berthold to take her into the forest and kill her. He takes a pig's heart back to Brangomar to show that he has performed the deed, and Snow White is led by the birds to the house of the seven dwarfs. (Disney acknowledged having been influenced by this in his production.) There follow the familiar attempts to kill Snow White with a poisoned comb and apple. The dwarfs jar the casket and dislodge the unswallowed apple from her throat just in time to prevent Florimond from slaying Brangomar, who is turned into a peacock instead.

COMMENTARY: The stage and screen career of Marguerite Clark (1883–1940) was managed by her sister Cora; the family had suffered financial reverses, and Marguerite made it no secret that she was in the theater to earn a living. She also admitted that she greatly preferred stage to screen but had adopted the latter because Adolph Zukor offered her so much more money than Broadway. Between 1914 and 1921 her popularity was very great. In the contest run by *Motion Picture Magazine* in 1918, she was less than 20,000 votes behind Mary Pickford, whom she always called her favorite screen star.

She was a tiny, graceful, slightly whimsical person, with a cool, crisp sweetness about her. She brought to the screen the technical skill her stage experience in both musicals and straight plays had taught her (she had had far more Broadway assignments than Mary Pickford), but though she was warmly admired by a large and devoted public which included George Jean Nathan, H. L. Mencken, and Sarah Bernhardt, she never matched Mary's hold upon the primal emotions.

Snow White first meets Prince Florimond hunting in the woods, and begs him not to kill his prey.

All this meant, inevitably, that her personality was exactly right for fairy tales, and since the screen can embrace fairy lore much more comfortably than the stage, it is not surprising that—barring her unquestioned masterpiece, *Prunella*—*Snow White* and *The Seven Swans* should be the two of her 39 films that are most fondly remembered. They were the Christmas attractions in American film theaters in 1916 and 1917, respectively, and both had her favorite director, the veteran J. Searle Dawley, who, like his wife, loved her dearly and directed 16 of her pictures. She had done both *Prunella* and *Snow White* for Winthrop Ames at the Little Theatre, the latter at matinees and Saturday morning performances while playing with John Barrymore in *The Affairs of Anatol* on the regular schedule, making a total of 13 performances a week.

The film used some of Ames's stage décor and would probably seem to have a certain old-fashioned theatrical quality about it if we could see it today (so far as is known, none of Miss Clark's films are extant). Its seasonal quality was emphasized by having Santa Claus come down the chimney at the beginning, after which his gifts came to life to mark the transition to fairyland. The exteriors were filmed in the South and if moss hanging from trees was not associated with Christmas in the minds of most moviegoers, it was still undeniably picturesque. (*E. W.*)

Above: "Snow White's hunger causes her to eat of the Dwarfs' prepared supper." Below: And Snow White and Prince Florimond lived happily ever after . . .

PANTHEA

A Selznick Pictures production. Released in January, 1917. 5 reels.

Producers: Joseph Schenck and Lewis J. Selznick. Director: Allan Dwan. Screenplay: Mildred Considine (based on the play by Monckton Hoffe). Photography: Roy F. Overbaugh. Assistant Directors: Erich von Stroheim and Arthur Rosson.

CAST: Norma Talmadge (*Panthea Romoff*); Earle Foxe (*Gerard Mordaunt*); L. Rogers Lytton (*Baron de Duisitor*); George Fawcett (*Chief of Police*); Murdock McQuarrie (*The Secret Agent*); Erich von Stroheim; Norbert Wicki; William Abbington; Winifred Harris; Elaine Persey; Stafford Windsor; Dick Rosson; Frank Currier; Herbert Barry; Jack Meredith; Henry Thorpe; William Lloyd; J. S. Furey.

SYNOPSIS: Panthea, a young Russian musician suspected of revolutionary activity, flees to England, where she marries a young composer. In Paris his failure to get his opera produced so works upon his health and spirits that his life is despaired of. One man, the Baron de Duisitor, who has already been responsible for Panthea's troubles in Russia, has the power to satisfy her husband's ambition, and he agrees to do so if Panthea will pay the price that Scarpia requires of Tosca. Though she loathes him, she agrees for her husband's sake, but when the latter learns what has happened, he is not pleased. The Baron expires of a heart attack, but Panthea is accused of having killed him. The end of the picture finds her reconciled with her husband, on the way to Siberian exile but hopeful of pardon through English diplomatic pressure.

COMMENTARY: Norma Talmadge (1897–1957), who, during her years of fame, was neither ingénue nor vampire woman, was one of the brightest stars of the silent screen. Unfortunately Joseph M. Schenck allowed her negatives to decay; consequently, while everybody can still see her sister Constance as the Mountain Girl in *Intolerance*, one can see very little of her, and all the wise men will tell you that she has been forgotten. Yet, after publishing *The Movies in the Age of Innocence*, I received more mail about her than about any other star, and this in spite of her not having been featured in the book, though all my references to her were friendly.

She began with Vitagraph, played with Florence Turner, whom she worshipped, in *A Dixie Mother*, in 1910, and, as noted elsewhere, rode with Sydney Carton to the guillotine in 1911. She was in *The Battle Cry of Peace* in 1915 and, after leaving Vitagraph, in *Captivating Mary Carstairs* and *The Social Secretary*. In 1916 she signed up with Lewis J. Selznick's Select Pictures and became associated with Schenck, whom she married and who supervised her films, which were released first through Select, then First National, and finally United Artists. *Panthea* and *Poppy* opened the procession; in the latter she first appeared with her best leading man, Eugene O'Brien. There followed *The Forbidden City, The Passion Flower, The Sign on the Door, Smilin' Through, Ashes of Vengeance, Within the Law, Graustark, Secrets, Kiki, Camille,* and others.

Despite, or because of, its delicate (or indelicate) subject matter, *Panthea* was a triumph, the first film in which a great star revealed her potential. "It is one of the best photoplays in screen history," declared Julian Johnson,

Director Allan Dwan discusses the production with Frank Currier, Norma Talmadge, L. Rogers Lytton, and Earle Foxe.

finding in the star "a verve, abandon and surety which denominates her queen of our younger silver sheet emotionalists. There is no [other] woman on the depthless stage who can flash from woe to laughter and back again with the certitude of this particular Talmadge." He returned to the theme in his annual review of the year's films: "Miss Talmadge has emerged from nervous, angular girlhood to emotional heights. Her performances of Panthea and Poppy, sweeping the whole gamut from childish playfulness to mature tragedy, are the feats of a virtuoso, ringing true in every tone." Edward Weitzel took only one exception: "The burden of acting borne by Norma Talmadge in *Panthea* would tax the ability of an emotional actress of the highest rank. The star of the screen play never suggests the land of her supposed nativity or the more erotic type which Mme. Petrova [who had done the play on the stage] associated with the character; but she does sound every emotion that stirs the heart of this woman who makes the supreme sacrifice out of unselfish love, and wins additional sympathy by reason of her youth, comeliness and the excellence of her histrionic method."

Norma Talmadge's career ended in 1930 with *Du Barry, Woman of Passion*. Allegedly, her voice was unsuited to the talkies, and the picture was quite dreadful. Among movie historians one parrot has echoed another in croaking out this song until it is now probably useless to object. But the truth of the matter is that there was nothing much wrong with the Talmadge voice (I can think of a number of ladies who made the transition from silence to sound, or even came in with the sound era, whose vocalism was never confused with that of either Sarah Bernhardt or Julia Marlowe), and *Du Barry* was not really a bad film. It was simply an old-fashioned historical melodrama of a kind that happened not to be in vogue at the time. (*E. W.*)

Above: *The Baron, Mordaunt, and Panthea*. Below: *Panthea and the Baron*.

Above: *Panthea fights off the advances of Baron de Duisitor.* Below: *Panthea and Gerard Mordaunt.*

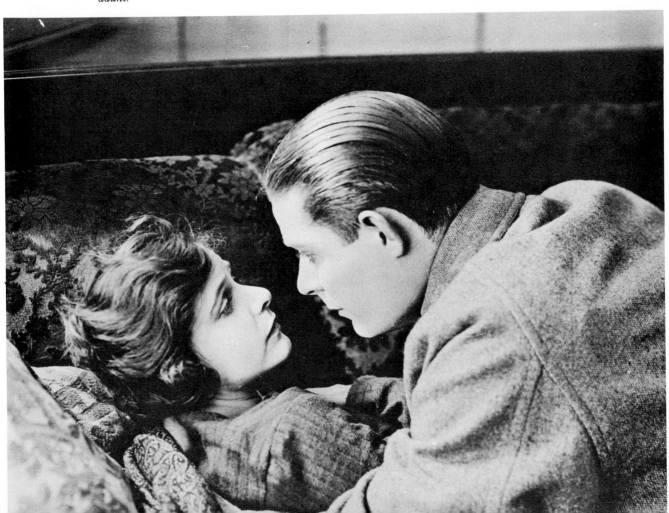

A POOR LITTLE RICH GIRL

An Artcraft production. Released March 5, 1917. 6 reels. Director: Maurice Tourneur. Screenplay: Ralph Spence and Frances Marion (based on the novel and play by Eleanor Gates). Photography: John van den Broek and Lucien Andriot. Art Director: Ben Carré. Assistant Director: M. N. Litson.

CAST: Mary Pickford (*Gwendolyn*); Madeline Traverse (*Her Mother*); Charles Wellesley (*Her Father*); Gladys Fairbanks (*Jane, the Nurse*); Frank McGlynn (*The Plumber*); Emile La Croix (*The Organ Grinder*); Marcia Harris (*Miss Royle, the Governess*); Charles Craig (*Thomas, the Footman*); Frank Andrews (*Potter, the Butler*); Herbert Prior (*The Doctor*); George Gernon (*Johnny Blake*); Maxine Hicks (*Susie May Squaggs*).

SYNOPSIS: Gwendolyn has all the luxuries money can buy, but her father is too busy making money and her mother spending it to pay much attention to her, and most of those employed to look after her are unsympathetic. Her parents come to their senses when she goes into delirium and nearly dies after having been given too much sleeping medicine by a nurse who wished to go out. "We have been fighting death itself," says her father when the long night ends, "and have learned what is truly precious. There is enough left for the life we are going to lead."

COMMENTARY: *A Poor Little Rich Girl*, which Viola Dana had done on the stage for Arthur Hopkins as his initial production in 1913 (it was the same year Mary Pickford did *A Good Little Devil* for Belasco), is an exquisite film—funny, touching, and mounted, directed, and photographed with great sensitivity by Maurice Tourneur and his associates, especially in the dream-delirium sequence. The French director had been working in the United States since 1914, but this was only the second of the many films he would make for the Paramount companies (the first had been *The Pride of the Clan*, also with Miss Pickford). In the opinion of this scribe, he was the finest of all early directors except Griffith.

Rich Girl has been chosen here as our second Pickford film not only because of its individual merits but because of the milestone it marked in her career. She had been young in all her feature films, but never so young as here, and unless you wish to exempt the screen version of *A Good Little Devil*, which hardly counted for anything, this was her first extended portrayal of a child. When the time inevitably came that she must make the transition to more mature roles, she would find the tremendous vogue of her portrayals of childhood no unmixed blessing. Meanwhile, however, years of unalloyed delight would intervene which nobody who lived through them could be persuaded to wish away.

Miss Pickford respected Tourneur's gifts, but she once told me she did not think him a good director for her because he did not understand American humor. The mud fight in *Rich Girl* (for so wistful and inhibited a child, Mary's Gwen was capable of a good deal of mischief) was included over his protest; to him mud was simply ugly. The really astonishing thing about the picture, however, is that neither the star nor her employers had any idea of the value of what they had turned out until its smashing success in the theaters made them aware of it. The actress indeed was as much discouraged about her career after completing *Rich Girl* as she ever was in her life. But *Wid's* called it the best thing she had ever done, and *Motography* thought her role in it brought out her "real genius," also praising Tourneur for the perfect atmosphere that he had achieved, while Edward Weitzel lauded Mary for her complete freedom "from the stock tricks of the ordinary child impersonator."

There are suggestions of both allegory and folklore in the dream sequence which brilliantly explores the mind of a child. Gwen has heard the servants call each other Two-Faced Thing, Snake-in-the-Grass, Big Ears, and Silly Ass, and in her dream they are literally that, though the Snake-in-the-Grass is not a real snake, and the Silly Ass she loves. She sees her father as "made of money" and her mother with a social "bee in her bonnet," she travels about "Robin Hood's Barn," and hears the "bears" growl in Wall Street. One scene shows "Where They Burn the Candle at Both Ends," another "The Forest Where The Lights Go When They Are Blown Out." All this, of course, was material much better adapted to the screen than it had been to the stage, and it was very fortunate that it fell into the hands of just the right people to make the most of it. (*E. W.*)

Above: *Gwendolyn wishes she could go out and play.* Below: *A discontented and unloved Gwendolyn in her nursery.*

"THEY FORGET I'VE GROWN UP"

MARY PICKFORD
IN
"POOR LITTLE RICH GIRL"

Above: "I don't like doctors," says Gwen to her father's medical friend. "They cut out little girls' appendixes and charge their papas a thousand dollars." Below: Filming the mud-fight sequence. Maurice Tourneur and his associates behind the camera.

A TALE OF TWO CITIES

A William Fox production. Released March 12, 1917. 7 reels.

Director: Frank Lloyd. Screenplay: Clara S. Beranger (based on the novel by Charles Dickens). Photography: Billy Foster.

(*A Tale of Two Cities* was reissued in 1920. The Charles Dickens novel was also filmed in 1935, by MGM, and in 1958, by J. Arthur Rank.)

CAST: William Farnum (*Charles Darnay/Sydney Carton*); Jewel Carmen (*Lucie Manette*); Charles Clary (*Marquis St. Evremonde*); Herschel Mayall (*Jacques DeFarge*); Rosita Marstini (*Madame DeFarge*); Josef Swickard (*Dr. Alexandre Manette*); Ralph Lewis (*Roger Cly*); William Clifford (*Gabelle*); Marc Robbins (*Mr. Jarvis Lorry*); Olive White (*Miss Pross*); William Louis (*Mr. Stryver*); Harry De Vere (*Gaspard*); Florence Vidor (*The Girl Who Rides to the Guillotine with Sydney Carton*).

SYNOPSIS: Charles Darnay, heir to the Evremonde fortune, is impelled by his sympathy with the people to renounce his inheritance in France and come to England, where he marries Lucie Manette, whose father, Dr. Manette, has been a Bastille prisoner. Lucie is also loved, hopelessly, by Sydney Carton, barrister and alcoholic. Darnay is falsely accused of treason, and Carton saves him by convincing the jury that since another man so closely resembles Darnay, the witness' positive identification of him cannot be trusted. When the Terror rages in France, Darnay goes to Paris on an errand of mercy and is arrested as an aristocrat. His first trial results in acquittal, but when Dr. Manette's old servant DeFarge produces a manuscript the doctor had written in prison, cursing the Evremondes to the last of their race, he is condemned to the guillotine. His devotion to Lucie leads Carton to make use of a hold he has over one of the guards to visit Darnay in his cell, where he drugs him, changes clothes with him, and has him placed in the coach to return to England while Carton dies in his place.

COMMENTARY: When it comes to *A Tale of Two Cities*, the present scribe has difficulty avoiding autobiography. Vitagraph's three-reel 1911 production was both my first "feature" and my introduction to the work of Charles Dickens, which was to be one of the prime literary passions of my life. In those days the rule was three reels of film and an "illustrated song" for a nickel. Theaters did not advertise, and they changed the bill every day. On the Saturday night my mother and I walked through Douglas Park to the little Acme Theater on Ogden Avenue in Chicago, we were simply going to the movies, with no idea of the special treat in store for us. When we arrived, we found *three* of Vitagraph's distinctive and beautiful posters before the theater, one for each reel; *A Tale of Two Cities* was the whole bill. It was one of the magical nights of my life, and I never ceased to cherish it in memory. I cannot honestly say that when Blackhawk Films found reels 2 and 3 and I had the privilege of writing an historical introduction to the edition which they brought out for collectors, I then saw the film with quite the same eyes that had beheld it in 1911; but enough continuity had been preserved so that I felt I had the privilege of reliving a part of my life.

The novel was not filmed again, in this country at least, until the Frank Lloyd production of 1917 that is the sub-

Sydney Carton.

ject of this notice. I do not believe that William Farnum was a better Carton than Maurice Costello had been (he was pretty robust and "wholesome" for the role), and I am not sure that Jewel Carmen was any lovelier than Florence Turner, whose only fault was that she was made to faint too often. But the later players were working on an immensely larger canvas, with far more attention paid to historical verisimilitude, and they had much better opportunities to flesh out their roles. A production of a major work of art in three reels always had a tendency to turn into a series of "illustrations" rather than a progressively unfolding conception; this was quite as true of Vitagraph's *Vanity Fair* and *As You Like It* as of *A Tale of Two Cities*.

Farnum had another advantage over Costello: technology had now developed to the point where it was possible for him to enact both Carton and Darnay, on Carton's physical resemblance to whom the plot turns. Fortunately Vitagraph had had an actor named Leo Delaney who sufficiently resembled Costello to make the substitution of one for the other believable with the aid of a little "poetic license"; without this, they could hardly have made the picture at all. Incidentally, it is interesting to note that when MGM made the 1935 version, they did not allow Ronald Colman to play both parts because they felt the audience could not be moved by the spectacle of a man dying for himself.

As the cast shows, the Farnum-Lloyd film retained all the important characters except Jerry Cruncher, though the Miss Pross of the film was far from Dickens' conception. Florence Vidor repeated screen history by the strong impression she made as the girl who rides to the guillotine with Carton, for young Norma Talmadge had done the same thing in 1911. In retrospect, Miss Vidor's success is far more comprehensible, for Norma comes and goes with such speed that one wonders how anybody could either have noticed or remembered her. (*E. W.*)

Above: *Dr. Manette hailed by the Revolutionary mob after his liberation from the Bastille.* Below:
Lucie, Miss Pross, Jarvis Lorry, and Charles Darnay.

WILLIAM FOX
PRESENTS
WILLIAM FARNUM
IN

DIRECTED BY
FRANK LLOYD

FOX FILM

Above: *Charles Darnay with Lucie Manette.* Below: *The victims of the Revolution on their way to the guillotine.*

THE SPIRIT OF '76

A Continental Producing Company production. World premiere: Orchestra Hall, Chicago, June, 1917. Los Angeles premiere: Clune's Auditorium, November 28, 1917. 12 reels (12,000 ft.). (Reissued in 1921 by the All-American Film Company.)

Producer: Robert Goldstein. Director: George Siegmann. Screenplay: Virginia Tyler Hudson. Assistant Director: Carl Leviness.

CAST: Adda Gleason (*Catherine Montour*); Howard Gaye (*Lionel Esmond*); Jack Cosgrove (*George III*); George Cheeseborough (*Walter N. Butler*); Noah Beery (*George Washington*); Jane Novak; Babe Lawrence; Dark Cloud; W. Freeman; Jack McCready.

SYNOPSIS: Catherine Montour, a half-Indian, has tremendous influence with Britain's George III and conspires against the American colonists to become Queen of America. She falls in love with Lionel Esmond, with whom she plots for her goal, only to discover just as they are about to be married that he is her brother. In the meantime, she has fallen out of favor with the King, and the American Revolution has dashed her hopes for an American monarchy. A number of historical events are featured, including Patrick Henry's speech before the Virginia House of Burgesses, Paul Revere's ride, the signing of the Declaration of Independence, Washington at Valley Forge, and Lord Chatham's death.

COMMENTARY: It is stories such as the one involving *The Spirit of '76* which make film history so fascinating. For here is a lost and forgotten film that created more of a stir in its day than many famous productions of the teens.

The Spirit of '76 was produced by Robert Goldstein, a tailor by profession, who supplied many of the costumes for *The Birth of a Nation* and who was also one of that film's financial backers. In the summer of 1916, he decided to embark on his own film production, for which he hired George Siegmann, a member of Griffith's stock company, as director, and another Griffith player, Howard Gaye, to be leading man. The theme of his film was the American War of Independence, but told with a decidedly anti-British slant. This would have been perfectly acceptable— accurate, as well, some might say—had not America been about to enter the war in Europe on the side of the British.

The film opened in Chicago, with its huge German population a safe bet for anti-British propaganda, to fairly favorable reviews. The critic in *Motography* (June 23, 1917) commented, "The picture contains a number of splendid moments and a great deal of narrative neither convincing nor interesting," while *Exhibitor's Trade Review* (June 9, 1917) wrote, "It has some truly wonderful moments and should cause the red blood of any American to tingle."

There were some censorship problems even in Chicago, but they were as nothing compared to the problems the film ran into in Los Angeles. Two days after its opening there, Federal officers seized the film and charged Goldstein with violation of the Espionage Act. The courts found that *The Spirit of '76* was "designed and intended to arouse antagonism, hatred and enmity between the American people and the people of Great Britain," and Goldstein was sentenced to a hefty prison term and a $5,000 fine. In a scathing editorial, *Photoplay* (August, 1918) called Goldstein "a bumptious ignoramus, more fool than villain, who mistook greedy aggressiveness for talent and business energy."

Tempers cooled with the ending of hostilities, and Goldstein was released after serving only one year of his prison sentence. He reissued the film in 1921, and Edward Weitzel's comment on that reissue in *The Moving Picture World* (August 6, 1921) perhaps best sums up the artistic worth of *The Spirit of '76*: "Up to the present this country has not attached a prison sentence to artistic crimes. Offenses against good taste and common sense bring no greater penalty than loss of patronage. This is fortunate for Mr. Robert Goldstein. He has ground out a crude concoction of fact and fiction, purporting to deal with some of the most momentous episodes in American history, and filled it with astonishing and mirthful anachronisms, with a few anachronisms thrown in for good measure." (A. S.)

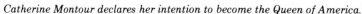
Catherine Montour declares her intention to become the Queen of America.

Above: *One of the historical tableaux that were pictured throughout* THE SPIRIT OF '76. *Below: The brutal knife fight between Walter Butler and an Indian.*

POLLY OF THE CIRCUS

A Goldwyn Features Corporation production. Released September 9, 1918. 8 reels.

Directors: Charles Horan and Edwin L. Hollywood. Screenplay: Adrian Gil Speare and Emmett Campbell Hall (based on the stage play by Margaret Mayo). Art Director: Everett Shinn.

(*Polly of the Circus* was remade by MGM in 1932 with Clark Gable and Marion Davies, under the direction of Alfred Santell.)

CAST: Mae Marsh (*Polly*); Vernon Steele (*The Minister*); Charles Riegel (*Deacon Strong*); Wellington Playter (*Jim*); Charles Eldridge (*Toby*); George Trimble (*Owner of the Circus*); Lucille La Verne and Dick Lee (*The Minister's Black Servants*); John Carr, Mildred Call, and Stephen Carr (*The Children*); Lucile Satterthwaite; J. B. Hollis; Isabel Vernon; Viola Compton.

SYNOPSIS: Polly, a circus rider, is injured while the show is playing in a small town, and taken to the home of the local minister, who soon falls in love with her. Hypocritical Deacon Strong disapproves of Polly and wants her to leave town. In the meantime, Polly learns of the illness of Toby, the circus clown, and enters her horse in the county-fair race to raise money for Toby's medical care. She beats the deacon's entry in the race, but it is too late, for Toby has died. By threatening to have the minister removed unless Polly leaves, the deacon rids the town of her, and it is not until a year later, when the circus revisits the town, that the minister learns the truth of the situation, and takes Polly back, despite the narrow-minded townspeople.

COMMENTARY: In the fall of 1916, Samuel Goldwyn— then Samuel Goldfish—established the Goldwyn Motion Picture Company, in association with Archie and Edgar Selwyn, Margaret Mayo, and Arthur Hopkins. In his autobiography, *Behind the Screen* (published by George H. Doran in 1923), Goldwyn noted that at the time of the formation of his company, "it was the player, not the play, which was the thing," and thus he determined to engage the leading actresses from stage and screen to star in his productions. From the theater, Goldwyn signed Jane Cowl, Maxine Elliott, Madge Kennedy, and Mary Garden, and from other film producers he lured away Mae Marsh and Mabel Normand. The results of his efforts were far from successful. Madge Kennedy was the only stage star to make a sizable impression in films, Mabel Normand suddenly ceased to be funny, and Mae Marsh, while still giving worthwhile performances, seemed ill at ease without the guidance of her mentor, D. W. Griffith.

The first Goldwyn production, *Polly of the Circus*, was filmed at a studio in Fort Lee, New Jersey, and scripted by Margaret Mayo, the wife of Edgar Selwyn. For Mae Marsh it was a happy time, not so much because of the production or the large salary she was receiving from Samuel Goldwyn, but because she met Goldwyn's director of publicity, Louis Lee Arms, whom she subsequently mar-

"Worthy of considerable attention is the appearance of an entire circus in a great many of the scenes," wrote Peter Milne in "Motion Picture News" (September 22, 1917). "It is a small town circus and so nothing might be lost in the way of sincerity and faithfulness of detail."

ried. Goldwyn was less happy; in his autobiography he noted that Mae Marsh "seemed incapable of any notable achievement when removed from the galvanizing influence of Griffith." The critics, such as Peter Milne in *Motion Picture News* (September 22, 1917), might comment that "Miss Marsh again demonstrates her right to be termed the best actress of the shadow stage," but the public showed a singular lack of interest.

Why, therefore, is *Polly of the Circus* an important production? The answer is simple; because it was the first independent filmmaking venture for both Mae Marsh and Samuel Goldwyn, and because it started Goldwyn on an illustrious producing career, which, despite a number of early disasters, was to continue for the next forty years. For the critic of the New York *Times* (September 10, 1917), "The first release, while not so noteworthy as to elevate Goldwyn immediately above all its competitors, is at least a careful and painstaking piece of work." Here is a comment that might well apply to the producer's work through the years. There is, of course, another reason for the importance of *Polly of the Circus*, and the other productions which followed. Thanks to them, Samuel Goldfish took a new name, a name that was to become as familiar to filmgoers as Louis B. Mayer's or Jack Warner's. (*A. S.*)

Above: *Polly and friend. (Lillian Gish once commented that Mae Marsh was the only actress of whom she was ever jealous.)* Below: *A delightful shot of Mae Marsh as Polly, which captures the natural, homely quality of her looks.*

BARBARY SHEEP

An Artcraft production. Released by Paramount, September 10, 1917. 6 reels.

Director: Maurice Tourneur. Screenplay: Charles Maigne (based on the novel by Robert Hichens). Photography: John van den Broek. Art Director: Ben Carré.

CAST: Elsie Ferguson (*Lady Kathryn Wyverne*); Lumsden Hare (*Sir Claude Wyverne*); Pedro de Cordoba (*Benchaalal*); Macy Harlan (*Achmed, a Native Guide*); Alex Shannon (*The Mad Marabout*); Maude Ford (*The Innkeeper*).

SYNOPSIS: The sportsman Sir Claude Wyverne and his bored wife Lady Kathryn come to Algeria, he to hunt Barbary sheep, she in the hope of finding romance. It appears in the person of one Benchaalal of the Algerian cavalry, but while her interest in him does not run beyond the length of an indiscreet flirtation, he is as much attracted by her jewels as her person; nor is he averse to using abduction to possess himself of both. Sir Claude is about to rescue his wife by killing Benchaalal when a "mad marabout" who has an old score to settle does the job for him. We are left with the feeling that the adventure has brought husband and wife together in a new understanding.

COMMENTARY: Elsie Ferguson (1883–1961), an established stage star, came to the screen with *Barbary Sheep* and continued to appear in films produced by the Paramount organization until 1922. Her patrician beauty, sensitiveness, and emotional power all proved valuable elements in her success. Maurice Tourneur directed her in four of her first six pictures, and though *Barbary Sheep* was not necessarily the best (she would later draw upon writers as much superior to the author of *The Garden of Allah* as Ibsen and Sudermann), it still provided a glamorous curtain raiser for her, as well as offering something of a preview of what we might expect in the day of the sheiks, which would soon be upon us.

Randolph Bartlett, in *Photoplay Magazine*, thought her cold, reserving his praise for Tourneur and his associates. "Never having visited the Sahara, we hesitate to say that the scenes are true to geographical fact. They are better than that. They transport one to Sahara, whether or not he knows the fauna and flora by their front names and telephone numbers. Any carpenter can build you a rock that looks like any rock in the Sahara. It takes an artist to build a rock that you *feel* belongs in Sahara." But Bartlett's seems to have been a minority view so far as the star was concerned. *The New York Dramatic Mirror* found her acting "with restraint and feeling" in "a most auspicious debut," while *The Moving Picture World* saw her bringing out Lady Kathryn's "conflict of emotions" with "a skill that has seldom been approached by actresses used to the picture camera and its exorbitant demands." (*E. W.*)

Lady Kathryn and Benchaalal, "the dark-skinned officer whose eyes gleam as they alight upon the sparkling diamond necklace about her throat."

Above: *Achmed and Lady Wyverne.* Below: *Lady Wyverne discovers the seamier side to her "dream of romance" of the Arab world.*

THE COUNTESS CHARMING

A Paramount-Artcraft production. Released September 23, 1917. 5 reels (4,459 ft.).

Director: Donald Crisp. Screenplay: Gardner Hunting (based on the story "Mrs. Raffles' Career," by Gelett Burgess and Carolyn Wells). Photography: Saxon Dean. Assistant Director: Claude Mitchell.

CAST: Julian Eltinge (*Stanley Jordan/Countess Raffelski*); Florence Vidor (*Betty Lovering*); Edythe Chapman (*Mrs. Lovering*); Tully Marshall (*Dr. John Cavendish*); Mabel Van Buren (*Mrs. John Vandergraft*); Gustav von Seyffertitz (*John Vandergraft*); Billy Elmer (*Detective Boyle*); Mr. and Mrs. George Kuwa.

SYNOPSIS: Stanley Jordan is introduced to the North Shore social colony by his friend Dr. Cavendish, but he is insulted by John Vandergraft and his wife, the undisputed leader of society. Mrs. Vandergraft brings pressure to bear on Mrs. Lovering to prevent Jordan from seeing her daughter Betty, with whom he has fallen in love and whom he has been aiding in collecting funds for the Red Cross. In retaliation, Jordan adopts the disguise of the Countess Raffelski, and is soon the season's sensation, while at the same time robbing the socialites of their valuables and turning over the proceeds to the Red Cross. By chance, Jordan stumbles upon a stock-market fraud perpetrated by Vandergraft, and is able to expose him and bring about the downfall of Mrs. Vandergraft, but at the same time he is almost caught by the police. His female career at an end, Jordan arranges for Countess Raffelski to have a fatal accident, and confesses all to Betty, who forgives him and agrees to become his bride.

COMMENTARY: It is curious that in an age where transvestism and female impersonation are commonplace, no one recalls Julian Eltinge, a man who was undoubtedly the greatest female impersonator of the American stage—the only performer remotely comparable in appeal is the British impersonator Danny La Rue—and who starred in a number of highly successful features in the late teens and early Twenties. Not that there was apparently anything effeminate about Julian Eltinge; as Ruth Gordon recalled, he was "as virile as anybody virile." One critic suggested that female impersonator was a misnomer, because, in fact, Eltinge was an impersonator of women—and there was nothing female about him. He was an impersonator who delighted in productions which required him to don female apparel for a very definite purpose, and then to discard it at the denouement of the work. He would never portray a woman just for the sake of portraying a woman, and, unlike today's best-known female impersonators, his act did not rely on second-rate imitation of leading female stars.

Aside from a brief appearance in *How Molly Made Good*, a novelty subject featuring a host of theatrical celebrities, produced by Burns Mantle in 1915, Julian Eltinge made his screen debut in *The Countess Charming*, a comedy-drama that poked subtle fun at social snobbery and the needs of the rich to adopt a suitable charity with which to be involved, in this case the American Red Cross. The plot revolved around Eltinge's female impersonation, and has definite links to Robin Hood, Zorro, and, of course, Raffles. When the star first decides upon his female disguise, he declares, "I'm a regular knight-errant. These gowns are my coat—of female!" Despite Julian Eltinge's being somewhat past his prime, *The Countess Charming* proved successful both critically and commercially. Randolph Barlett in *Photoplay* (December, 1917) described it as "great fun," while Louis Reeves Harrison in *The Moving Picture World* (October 6, 1917) thought it "bound to charm, and in that respect it stands unique among the class of production known as a 'vehicle,' principally because it rises out of the vehicle class at times, and because of the remarkable personality of Julian Eltinge."

The Countess Charming was followed by other Eltinge vehicles: *The Clever Mrs. Carfax* (1917), *The Widow's Might* (1918), and *An Adventuress* (1920), among others. It is not surprising that producers were happy to turn out films such as *The Countess Charming*, which took a mere month to shoot and edit, and cost, in all, a little over fifty thousand dollars. Julian Eltinge's last silent feature was *Madame Behave* for the Christie Comedy Company in 1925. (As I have commented elsewhere, Al Christie's penchant for dressing men in women's clothing and vice versa is very obvious from a study of the subject matter of his short films, not to mention two productions of *Charley's Aunt!*) In 1931, Eltinge starred in a Poverty Row production, *Madame Behave*, released by Artclass Pictures, and in 1940 he made a cameo appearance in *If I Had My Way*. Eltinge died the following year, on March 7, 1941, at the age of 58. (*A. S.*)

Above: *George Kuwa, with Julian Eltinge as Stanley Jordan: "I'm a regular knight-errant. These gowns are my coat—of female!" Below: "Countess Raffelski," whom Louis Reeves Harrison in "The Moving Picture World" (October 6, 1917) described as "an interesting human creature as woman would be if she grew up the way she ought."*

Above: *Countess Raffelski impresses the social set.* Below: *Countess Raffelski, John Vandergraft, and Dr. Cavendish form the center of the crowd.*

STELLA MARIS

An Artcraft production. Released January 21, 1918. 6 reels.

Director: Marshall Neilan. Screenplay: Frances Marion (based on the novel by William J. Locke). Photography: Walter Stradling. Art Director: Wilfred Buckland. Assistant Director: Nat Deverich.

(*Stella Maris* was remade by Universal in 1926 with Mary Philbin, under the direction of Charles Brabin.)

CAST: Mary Pickford (*Stella Maris/Unity Blake*); Conway Tearle (*John Risca*); Marcia Manon [Camille Ankewich] (*Louise Risca*); Ida Waterman (*Lady Blount*); Herbert Standing (*Lord Blount*); Josephine Crowell (*Aunt Gladys Linden*); Mrs. Coonleu (*The Nurse*); Teddy, the Mack Sennett Dog (*The Dog*).

SYNOPSIS: Stella Maris, an invalid confined to her bed, lives surrounded by luxury and the devotion of Lord and Lady Blount and her "Great High Belovedest," John Risca. She is ignorant of all the evils of life. But Risca has a wife, an alcoholic maniac who, in a drunken rage, beats Unity Blake, an ugly, slightly deformed little slavey, nearly to death. Risca makes himself responsible for Unity and she becomes deeply devoted to him and Stella. Stella regains her health and her power of locomotion and is crushed upon learning that the world is not what she had believed it to be. She also now knows that she loves John Risca with a woman's love and that his wife stands in the way of their happiness. Unity too loves Risca, but realizing the hopelessness of her passion, and out of pure devotion to John and Stella, she goes to Mrs. Risca's flat, where she shoots her and herself, thus making it possible for John and Stella to wed.

COMMENTARY: *Stella Maris* is said to have been put into production during Adolph Zukor's absence from the studio, so that when, returning, he ran into Mary Pickford on the lot in her Unity makeup, he was nearly overcome; nor did he find it at all reassuring when she told him not to mind since she died in the course of the picture! It is arguably her greatest film. It was made late in 1917, probably her greatest single year, during which she ap-peared in six films, of which three—*A Poor Little Rich Girl*, *The Little American*, and *Rebecca of Sunnybrook Farm*—were smash hits.

Her appearance in a dual role, both characters appearing on the screen together, was in itself a technical triumph in those days, but the nature of the Unity character was even more sensational. Mary's fans were allowed to see her as Stella in all her curls and beauty; as Unity she was more than a little grotesque, yet she never forfeited audience sympathy. Her performance was never the "stunt" it might so easily have become with a lesser artist, but a genuine characterization, the portrait of one set apart, yet, for all that, as Joseph Conrad might say, "one of us."

Contemporary reviewers were ecstatic, declaring that the film brought out aspects of Mary's art that had lain dormant since Biograph days. *Motion Picture* called the film her "greatest personal triumph"; *Photoplay* prophesied that her public would never again be satisfied to see her in roles in which she was not permitted to act. In part all this was due to the myopia that causes persons who lack the capacity for fine discriminations to appreciate what is generally called "character" acting while remaining blind to the differences in shading between not wholly dissimilar "straight" roles, which, as any actor who knows his business can tell you, are much more difficult to do. It is true, nevertheless, that Miss Pickford had had a chance to portray a much wider variety of characters in her Biographs than had come her way since she had acquired a world following. Her newer fans were much more interested in her own charms than in the characters she portrayed.

In any event, both she and the film deserved all the praise they received. Marshall Neilan turned in a most workmanlike piece of direction. Marcia Manon made a strong impression in the hateful role of the cruel, drunken wife, which she acted to the hilt. Conway Tearle gave one of the most winning of his always polished performances as John Risca. Ida Waterman, who played older women with so much dignity in several Pickford films, was at her best, and even Mack Sennett's Teddy added to his following. But most of all *Stella Maris* was Mary Pickford's own never-to-be-forgotten triumph. (*E. W.*)

Above: *Mary Pickford as Stella Maris.* Below: *Mary Pickford as both Unity Blake and Stella Maris. In one scene, one figure was made to pass behind the other.*

MARY PICKFORD
IN
"STELLA MARIS"

THE BOTTLE! THE ORIGIN OF ALL HER WOES,
AND HER SEMI-INSANITY.

Above: *Unity Blake and Mrs. Risca: "The bottle! The origin of all her woes, and her semi-insanity."* Below: *Stella, recovered but disillusioned, with John Risca and Lady Blount.*

Above: *Stella, with John Risca, in the garden.* Below: *Unity, with gun poised, ready to shoot Mrs. Risca.*

THE BLUE BIRD

An Artcraft production. Released by Paramount, March 31, 1918. 6 reels.

Director: Maurice Tourneur. Screenplay: Charles Maigne (based on the stage play by Maurice Maeterlinck). Photography: John van den Broek. Art Director: Ben Carré.

(*The Blue Bird* was remade twice by 20th Century-Fox: in 1940 by director Walter Lang and in 1976 by director George Cukor.)

CAST: Robin Macdougall (*Tyltyl*); Tula Belle (*Mytyl*); Edwin E. Reed (*Daddy Tyl*); Emma Lowry (*Mummy Tyl*); William J. Gross (*Gaffer Tyl*); Florence Anderson (*Granny Tyl*); Edward Elkas (*Berlingot*); Katherine Bianchi (*Berlingot's Daughter*); Lillian Cook (*Fairy Berylune*); Charles Ascot (*Dog*); Tom Corless (*Cat*); S. E. Popapovitch (*Fire*).

SYNOPSIS: *The Blue Bird* is an allegorical fairy tale in which the Bird symbolizes happiness. Under the guidance of the Fairy Berylune, the children Tyltyl and Mytyl set out to find him, and their search leads them through many aspects of human experience. They even travel into the past to meet their dead grandparents and into the Palace of the Unborn, where they encounter those who still await their incarnation. They are accompanied in their quest by Bread, Milk, Water, Fire, Dog, Cat, etc. After their return home, they find the Blue Bird in their own kitchen, which is of course the point of the fable.

COMMENTARY: Maeterlinck's play *The Blue Bird* was produced for the first time in America at the New Theatre, New York, on October 1, 1910, and was accounted the Number One success of that ambitious and idealistic but ill-planned and ill-fated venture. The play was also widely read for many years.

If Maurice Tourneur's productions of it and *Prunella* had met the success they deserved, they might have pointed the way to a 1920s in which the screen might have been decorated by something better than sheiks and flappers and flaming youth. Edward Weitzel in *The Moving Picture World* could find no fault with *The Blue Bird* except that some of the transformations "could be quickened to advantage, and the spell of weirdness is occasionally absent." He saw in it "the simplicity of childhood and the wisdom of a deep but kindly philosophy," and prophesied that it would "appeal to every mind." *Photoplay* too carried the torch valiantly for "one of the most important productions ever made" and one "so beautiful, from beginning to end, that it stings the senses, awakening in the spectator esthetic emotions so long dormant, so seldom exercised, that the flashing light of the awakening is almost a surfeit of joy." But, alas for Weitzel's prophecy, one cannot appeal to a mind that is absent, and the reviewer in *Motion Picture Magazine* spoke for many: "Frankly *The Blue Bird* bored me. Seven reels of children trailing through fairy palaces with bread, water, light, and fire, that have been made to come to life, is frankly tedious on the screen." By 1920 Tourneur was writing me that he did not blame me for having been disappointed in some of his recent films. "So was I. Unfortunately, in this complex and fascinating business, there are so many elements to be considered that you don't always do what you want, but most of the time what you can."

It must be admitted, of course, that neither allegory nor fairy lore are for all markets, and even that Maeterlinckian symbolism is not for all those who may find wonder acceptable in other expressions. And, obviously, it would be a mistake to look to *The Blue Bird* for the dramatic force and continuity that other types of story could readily yield on screen. The values of the production were frankly moral and pictorial, and where these failed to appear, it was hopeless to look elsewhere for success. Nevertheless those who rejected them out of hand judged neither the film nor the director but themselves.

In one scene Tourneur used two beautiful naked children, a boy and a girl, to represent Sleep and Death. It is sad to record that at some point a mercifully unidentified prude cut the only close shot of them from what, so far as I know, is the only extant print of *The Blue Bird*, which is at Eastman House. (*E. W.*)

Tyltyl, Mytyl, and Mummy Tyl: "Christmas Eve—Mother Tyl puts the children to bed."

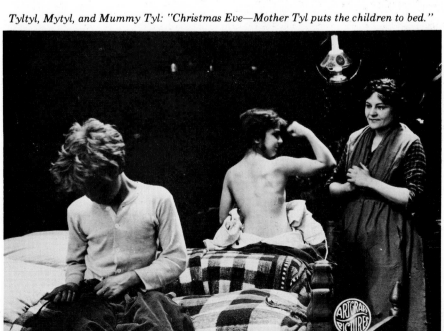

In the Palace of Night.

Above: *"In the Palace of Night." The nude Sleep and Death lie at the foot of the throne.* Below: *Berylune, Tyltyl, and Mytyl: "In the Enchanted Wood."*

In the Enchanted Wood.

Above: *"And this is the Palace of Happiness."* Below: *"Oh! Gaffer, your blackbird is now blue."*

PRUNELLA

A Famous Players-Lasky production. Released by Paramount, May 26, 1918. 5 reels.

Director: Maurice Tourneur. Screenplay: Charles Maigne (based on the stage play by H. Granville-Barker and Laurence Housman). Photography: John van den Broek. Art Director: Ben Carré.

CAST: Marguerite Clark (*Prunella*); Jules Raucourt (*Pierrot*); Harry Leoni (*Scaramel*); Isabel Berwin, Marcia Harris, and Nora Cecil (*The Aunts*); William J. Gross, A. Voorhes Wood, and Charles Hartley (*The Gardeners*); Arthur Kennedy (*The Gardeners' Boy*).

SYNOPSIS: With three maiden aunts, Prim, Prude, and Privacy, and their servants, Queer and Quaint, Prunella lives in the little house set in a Dutch garden from which her mother eloped with the "French gentleman-gardener" who put up the fountain-statue of Love that still stands in the garden. A troupe of mummers comes by. Despite all the aunts' care, Prunella meets and is captivated by Pierrot. That night he and his friends steal her away, and she becomes a member of their troupe. But Pierrot's heart lacks the faithfulness of Prunella's, and he soon tires of her. Three years later, all the aunts but one dead and the house sold, we find her stealing back to the now ruined garden. There a chastened Pierrot finds her, and the lovers are reconciled and reunited.

COMMENTARY: Film began as what is now called documentary, by photographing what happened instead of making it happen for the purpose of photographing it, and there have been dogmatists who have been prepared to insist that the medium is inevitably naturalistic. Yet what could be more authentically cinematic than the transformation of an ordinary pumpkin and other kitchen and barnyard articles into a coach and its accoutrements in Herbert Brenon's production *A Kiss for Cinderella?* In what other medium could this have been presented?

Nonrealism appeared very early and was industriously cultivated by the first real artist of the screen, Georges Méliès. It has been said that he discovered his métier accidentally when his camera jammed while he was photographing a street scene, so that when the film was developed a bus had been changed into a hearse. From here he went on to explore all the wonders of *A Trip to the Moon* and its many fellow productions.

The great success of *The Great Train Robbery* in 1903 powerfully strengthened the screen's commitment to naturalism, though it should not be forgotten that in *The Dreams of a Rarebit Fiend* (1906), Edwin S. Porter himself anticipated some of the devices that overwhelmed everybody as startling nonrealistic innovations when F. W. Murnau used them in 1925 in *The Last Laugh.* Despite Méliès' really brilliant example, however, "studio" productions have probably nowhere threatened to predominate in cinema except, for a time, during the golden age of the German film following World War I. In Fritz Lang's *Nibelungen* films, even the trees were "made," so that everything should be in key with everything else, with no intrusive nor accidental elements.

In this country, Douglas Fairbanks imitated the Germans in *The Thief of Bagdad* (1924), with distinguished success upon the whole, even going to the extent of buying Lang's *Destiny,* the principal single influence upon it, to

Prunella under the watchful eye of her three maiden aunts.

keep it off the American market, but probably the limits of stylization were achieved with Tourneur's *Prunella* and Nazimova's 1922 *Salome,* which had settings à la Beardsley by Valentino's wife, Natacha Rambova, and (uncredited) Harold Grieve.

Though *Salome* had its admirers, most viewers including this one thought it freakish. The star's unfitness for the role of the degenerate adolescent was colossal, and the film had an almost fatal influence upon her screen career. *Prunella,* though not a marked box-office success, was, on the other hand, a perfect thing in its way, and there is no film whose loss is more to be lamented. Tourneur himself rejoiced that he had been permitted to bring stylization to the screen, sounding "the note of fragile phantasy" in *The Blue Bird* and catching "the gossamer of whimsical romance" in *Prunella.*

Prunella was not a more beautiful film than *The Blue Bird* but it was more completely of a piece. If I may trust my memory, this was the only one of Tourneur's films into which nothing extraneous or "natural" was permitted to intrude. He had, of course, the good fortune of having found very distinguished material to work with. As both playwright and producer, Harley Granville-Barker was one of the great talents of the modern British drama, while his collaborator, Laurence Housman, was gifted as both writer and illustrator, being best known in the theater for *Victoria Regina.* Their play, partly in verse, is ballet-like in its movement, and Marguerite Clark had already given what was perhaps the performance of her life in it in Winthrop Ames's Little Theatre production. It is hard to believe, however, that any stage production could have achieved the beauty of the film; for once, Tourneur's unequaled pictorialism, his gentleness, sensitiveness, and moral refinement had all been perfectly accommodated. He and Charles Maigne had also contributed important material of their own (the heroine's role in the play, good as it is, is a very short one) by allowing us to see something of Prunella's life with the player troupe, which is only spoken of, not shown, in the play. (*E. W.*)

Above: *Pierrot paints to Prunella the world as it really is, and woos her with lurid song and fervent poetry.* Below: *Pierrot, Prunella and the troupe of mummers wander through strange lands. (As historian-critic Richard Koszarski has written, "Tourneur's fantasy landscape often explored the unreality of theatrical space . . . he even played games with the notion of the theater as life . . . or life as theater.")*

Above: *Prunella comes face to face with the realities of life. (In "Motion Picture Classic" of August, 1918, Frederick James Smith wrote, "Miss Clark's Prunella is a fascinating thing of thistledown, sympathetic and completely charming, and, we believe, the best film contribution of her career.")*
Below: *Pierrot and Prunella with the life-size figure of Cupid, sculptured by the gardener who eloped with Prunella's mother. To this figure the girl laments, "You spoke and all the world became a song, And all my heart a bird that heard its note."*

MICKEY

A Mabel Normand Feature Film Company production. Released by Western Import Company on a states-rights basis in the summer of 1918. 7 reels.

Producer: Mack Sennett. Director: F. Richard Jones. Based on a story by J. G. Hawks. Photography: Hans F. Koenekamp. Title song by Harry Williams.

CAST: Mabel Normand (*Mickey*); Louis [Lew] Cody (*Reggie Drake*); Tom Kennedy (*Tom Rawlins*); Laura La Varnie (*Mrs. Geoffrey Drake*); Wheeler Oakman (*Herbert Thornhill*); Minta Durfee (*Elsie Drake*); Minnie (*Minnie Ha Ha*); George Nichols (*Joe Meadows*); William Colvin (*The Butler*).

SYNOPSIS: The tomboy Mickey, who has been brought up by her father, a miner, and an old Indian woman, is sent to an aunt in the city to receive a proper education. But the aunt turns out to be an impecunious social climber and cold-hearted to boot. Her only interest is to marry her daughter to a wealthy man, Thornhill. Of course Thornhill is attracted to Mickey; so, too, is the unworthy Reggie. Both Mickey and Thornhill are valued and disvalued by the others as variant reports are received concerning their financial status. In the ensuing complications, a situation develops that causes Mickey to come to Thornhill's aid by masquerading as a jockey and riding in a race. She wins the race but is injured. After a final confrontation between Reggie and Thornhill, Mickey and the latter are united.

COMMENTARY: It is curious that despite her lasting fame and popularity, few of Mabel Normand's films have survived and only a handful of those that have give indication of her comic genius. Her one surviving Goldwyn production, *What Happened to Rosa* (1920), does not, nor do most of her extant Keystone shorts. Two features, *Mickey* and *The Extra Girl* (1923), hint at Mabel's talents, and illustrate to today's audiences why Mabel Normand deserves a pedestal only slightly lower than those reserved for Chaplin, Lloyd, Keaton, and Langdon, and far loftier than those of Larry Semon, Lloyd Hamilton, and the members of the Mack Sennett and Al Christie stock companies.

It can be no coincidence that both *Mickey* and *The Extra Girl* were directed by F. Richard Jones, a multi-talented, underrated technician, responsible for other Normand features in the Twenties (including *Molly O'* of 1921) and for *The Gaucho* (1928), the best of the later Fairbanks productions. Jones entered films in the Sennett cutting rooms, and by 1924 was supervising director and production manager for all Sennett releases. He later held a similar position with Hal Roach and must be given much of the credit for the early success of Our Gang, Charley Chase, and Laurel and Hardy comedies. At the time of *Mickey* he was 22.

In an effort to please his most important star, Mack Sennett had formed the Mabel Normand Feature Film Company in April of 1916. Mabel chose the story *Mickey* for her first semi-independent venture and Jones as her director. For reasons now unclear, but probably due to disagreements between director and producer—others, such as James Young, aside from Jones, had a hand in the direction—it was not until April 30, 1917 that *The Mack Sennett Weekly* announced: "The finishing touches are being put on the cutting of *Mickey*... upon which Mabel Normand has been working for eight months." Then Kessel and Bauman, Sennett's financial backers, took a look at the finished film, did not like what they saw, and shelved it, with the result that Mabel Normand left the Sennett Studios and signed what was to prove a disastrous contract with Goldwyn.

Mickey did not see the light of day until the summer of 1918, but when it did appear critical reaction was decidedly favorable. Most thought the story slight and drawn out—Frederick James Smith in *Motion Picture Classic* (October, 1918) suggested the film should have been released as a series of one-reel shorts—but all agreed that Mabel Normand's performance was a delight. Julian Johnson in *Photoplay* (April, 1919) wrote of Normand that "she is startling, vivacious, girlish, and always funny," while Peter Milne in *Motion Picture News* (August 3, 1918) commented, "In her role here Miss Normand does some real acting that makes one sit up and take notice."

The many sides of Mabel Normand's screen personality were seen to advantage in *Mickey*. Crude slapstick was represented by such scenes as the one in which a squirrel runs up inside Mabel's trouser leg. In an early scene, there is humor in the Pickford manner as Mabel enters a store with her dog, and the proprietor takes a dislike to the animal and vice versa. The tomboyish elements in Mabel's character were taken care of by a chase through a deserted house and a climactic horse-race sequence. Her natural grace and beauty were seen to advantage in a tastefully shot scene, shown at a distance, in which Mabel performs high dives in the nude. And there was even a hint of pathos. One need not look far for an explanation as to the quality of Mabel's performance. In a 1921 interview, F. Richard Jones explained, "I try to draw out the individual personalities of the players. And for this reason I never act out any of the play for them. As we pay for personality, why not develop it rather than endeavor to work it into something else." In *Mickey*, the director's style and the star's personality met in a perfect match. (*A. S.*)

Above: "It is neither exaggeration nor personal tribute," wrote Julian Johnson in "Photoplay" (September, 1916), "to say that Mabel Normand knows more about screen comedy, and has made better screen comedy, than any woman actively photographed." Below: Mickey and Reggie Drake, the villain. (Cody married Mabel in 1926 and remained with her until her death in 1930.)

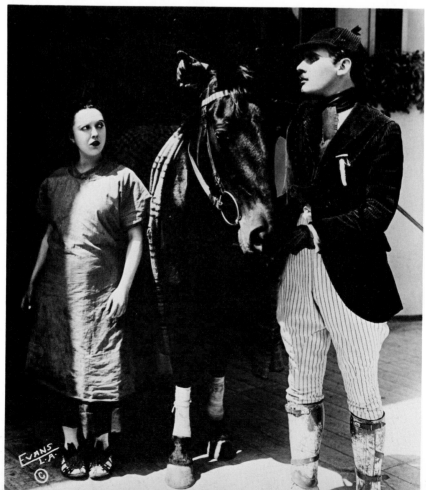

Above: *After Mickey is thrown from her horse, Thornhill (carrying her) and Tom Rawlins (right) attend to her.* Below: *A happy ending for hero and heroine, Thornhill and Mickey.*

THE HEART OF HUMANITY

A Universal-Jewel production. Released February 15, 1919. 9 reels.

Director: Allen Holubar. Screenplay: Allen Holubar and Olga Scholl. Photography: King D. Gray and A. McClain.

CAST: Dorothy Phillips (*Nanette*); William Stowell (*John Patricia*); Robert Anderson (*Paul Patricia*); Lloyd Hughes (*Jules Patricia*); Frank Braidwood (*Maurice Patricia*); George Hackathorne (*Louis Patricia*); Margaret Mann (*The Widow Patricia*); Walt Whitman (*Father Michael*); Pat O'Malley (*Clancy*); Erich von Stroheim (*Lieutenant von Eberhard*).

SYNOPSIS: Nanette, the niece of a patriarchal priest in rural Canada, weds John Patricia, one of five brothers, all of whom go to France in World War I. Greatly moved by what she learns of the sufferings of children in the war zone, she leaves her own child in charge of his grandmother and follows her husband to France as a Red Cross nurse. When the Germans capture the convent in which she has been caring for the children, she is attacked by Lieutenant von Eberhard, who had previously tried to win her by gentler means in Canada, but her husband arrives in time to save her. After the war they return to Canada with five refugee children.

COMMENTARY: Dorothy Phillips, a Baltimore girl who began with Essanay, and whose career continued at least to the end of the silents, is one of the once famous stars whom film history seems determined to ignore; nobody even seems to know whether she is living or dead. Yet in 1917 Julian Johnson was booming her along with Norma Talmadge: "Dorothy Phillips, as a dramatic actress, cannot be excelled today. She has poise, beauty, apparently inexhaustible reserve. She cannot, like Miss Talmadge, flash like lightning from laughter to tears and back again, but she has more sheer strength and drive." Frederick James Smith too found her "an actress of singular vividness."

The Heart of Humanity, directed by her husband, the late Allen Holubar, is today her best-remembered film. It was one of the big World War I pictures, though it had the misfortune not to be released until after the war was over. The title was obviously intended to recall *Hearts of the World,* as was Erich von Stroheim's familiar caricature of a degenerate German officer; at one point the heroine even temporarily loses command of her faculties. But if the film has the usual simplistic presentation of the war as a conflict between straight good and evil, it still strikes its own note in presenting a contrast between the peace of rural Canada and the agonies of the war zone, as well as in concentrating upon the fortunes of children rather than soldiers. Even more than the rest of the production, the scenes in which the children appear are "milked" for all the emotion they can be made to yield, and the captions are outrageously sentimental.

The battle scenes are impressive, but we nearly lose sight of the heroine while our attention is centered upon them. Indeed, considering the nature of the film and the amount of action included in it, Dorothy Phillips is allowed surprisingly little movement, and most of her best acting is confined to her close-ups. (*E. W.*)

In peaceful Canada. On the left Jules Patricia is nearest the camera and Lieutenant von Eberhard closest to the priest.

Above: *In the war zone: Nanette and John Patricia.* Below: *Nanette and her husband in the convent/child refuge.*

BROKEN BLOSSOMS

A D. W. Griffith production. Released by United Artists. New York premiere: George M. Cohan Theatre, May 13, 1919. 7 reels.

Director and Screenplay (based on the story, "The Chink and the Child," in *Limehouse Nights* by Thomas Burke): D. W. Griffith. Photography: G. W. "Billy" Bitzer. Special Effects: Hendrik Sartov. Additional Photography: Karl Brown. Film Editor: James Smith. Technical Adviser: Moon Kwan. Music Arranged by Louis F. Gottschalk and D. W. Griffith.

(*Broken Blossoms* was remade in England in 1936, starring Dolly Haas and Emlyn Williams under the direction of John Brahm.)

CAST: Lillian Gish (*Lucy Burrows*); Richard Barthelmess (*The Yellow Man* [*Cheng Huan*]); Donald Crisp (*Battling Burrows*); Arthur Howard (*His Manager*); Edward Peil (*Evil Eye*); George Beranger (*The Spying One*); Norman "Kid McCoy" Selby (*The Prizefighter*).

SYNOPSIS: Lucy, abused daughter of the small-time prizefighter Battling Burrows, "an abysmal brute from the jungles of East London," stumbles into the Limehouse curio shop of Cheng Huan after a particularly severe beating, and faints there. The idealism that impelled Cheng Huan to come to England to convert Westerners to Buddhism has long since been eroded, but he has admired Lucy from afar, and he treats her like a princess, surrounding her with beautiful objects and showing her the first kindness she has ever known. Through an informer, Battling learns where she is and goes to avenge his "honor." He does not find Cheng Huan, but he wrecks the room and drags the girl home, where he beats her to death. Cheng, having found his shrine violated, follows and kills him, after which he carries Lucy's body back to his room and there stabs himself.

COMMENTARY: If one were to select a single film to represent Lillian Gish's career, there is no question it would have to be *Broken Blossoms*. Her performance here stands with Mae Marsh's in *The Birth of a Nation* as one of the greatest emotional roles ever captured on celluloid. The quiet vulnerability she brings to the character of Lucy, the wondrous look of security in those wide eyes as she is taken in and cared for and cosseted by Richard Barthelmess' Chinese immigrant, the pitiful attempt at a smile by the use of the fingers to hold up the sides of her mouth have never been duplicated by screen actresses before or since.

But *Broken Blossoms* is far more than Lillian Gish's performance. It is a plea for tolerance as pertinent today as it was sixty years ago. It is poetry on film, poetry in the visual images and poetry in the titles. It is, in the words of Julian Johnson in *Photoplay* (August, 1919), "a great photoplay of insignificant title. It is the first genuine tragedy of the movies." *Tol'able David* aside, it probably presented Richard Barthlemess with the greatest acting role of his career, and the young player grasped the opportunity to give a sensitive and beautiful portrayal of a quiet and impassive Oriental whose love is as pure as Griffith's helplessly sentimental image of womanhood. Above all, it is D. W. Griffith, the master director, showing his consummate skill at producing a simple, intimate film which might reach the hearts of both the intelligentsia and the masses. Without *Intolerance's* mighty sets and thousands of extras and complex stories, *Broken Blossoms* makes a gentle, heart-rending plea for brotherly love. Griffith blended his ties with literature and Victorian morality with the most modern techniques available to the filmmaker, utilizing delicate tints and tones, and colored lights beamed directly onto the screen, to bring a new romanticism to the cinema.

Broken Blossoms opened the D. W. Griffith Repertory Season at New York's George M. Cohan Theatre on May 13, 1919. It was also the first Griffith film to be released by the newly formed United Artists. It served as a salute to the director's past work and a happy omen of things in store. And there were good films ahead for Griffith—*Way Down East, Orphans of the Storm, Isn't Life Wonderful, The Sorrows of Satan,* and *The Struggle,* perhaps all not recognized as such in Griffith's own lifetime—but there was also defeat and despair. Lillian Gish was to remain with Griffith for only two more years, and personal problems were to beset the director to such an extent that his career would suffer. All in all, *Broken Blossoms* might be viewed as a fitting close to the director's career in the teens. The star and director had worked well together for some seven years, and there was no reason to assume that they might not continue to turn out further great films in the years ahead. (*A. S.*)

Above: *Lucy, terrified of her brutal father, Battling Burrows, in the hovel they inhabit.* Below: *Cheng Huan with Lucy in the haven he has prepared for her.*

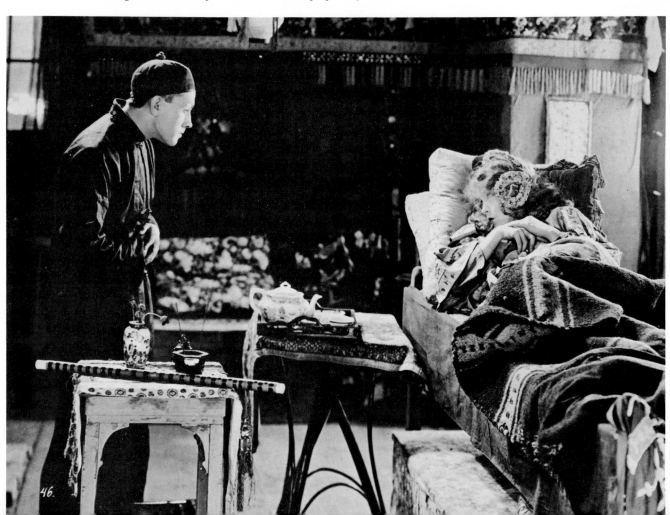

Above: *Lucy, in the famous closet scene. In a few moments, her father will break in the door and drag her out to beat her to death.* Below: *Cheng Huan's suicide, beside the dead Lucy, in his desecrated shrine.*

THE MIRACLE MAN

An Artcraft production. Released by Paramount, September 7, 1919. 7 reels.

Director and Screenplay (based on the story by Frank Packard and the stage play by George M. Cohan): George Loane Tucker. Subtitles: Wid Gunning. Art Titles: Ferdinand Pinney Earle. Photography; Philip E. Rosen and Ernest G. Palmer.

(*The Miracle Man* was remade by Paramount in 1932, with Sylvia Sidney, Chester Morris, and John Wray, under the direction of Norman McLeod.)

CAST: Thomas Meighan (*Tom Burke*); Betty Compson (*Rose*); Lon Chaney (*The Frog*); J. M. Dumont (*The Dope*); W. Lawson Butt (*Richard King*); Elinor Fair (*Claire King*); F. A. Turner (*Mr. Higgins*); Lucille Hutton (*Ruth Higgins*); Joseph J. Dowling (*The Patriarch, also known as "The Miracle Man"*).

SYNOPSIS: Tom Burke, his "girl" Rose, the "Frog," and the "Dope" are doing very well with a Chinatown racket when they learn of a deaf-blind Patriarch in a nearby town to whom healing of body and mind is being credited. Since the "Frog's" particular stunt is his ability to twist his body out of shape and then straighten up again, this seems a perfect set-up for them; once he has been spectacularly "cured," what may they not make by stage-managing the enterprise? To their astonishment, a young woman and a little boy experience real cures. Financially they accomplish far more than they had bargained for, but the Patriarch's goodness and the atmosphere in which they now live cuts the ground from under their feet and they find that they cannot live with themselves upon the old basis. The "Dope," having fought free of his addiction, finds a sweetheart and the "Frog" a "mother," while Tom and Rose replace their old lust with love.

COMMENTARY: *The Miracle Man* may have helped to convince the industry that a good picture could succeed without stars, yet it created three new ones. Thomas Meighan had long been a reliable and personable leading man (many must have remembered him in Blanche Sweet films at Lasky), but Betty Compson had only been an eyeful in Christie comedies, and though Lon Chaney had been in pictures for six years, he was nowhere so far as the average moviegoer was concerned.

Meighan, Chaney, and Miss Compson all had important careers; Tucker, for whom the film might have done much more, did not; he died at 49 in 1921. Both Julian Johnson and the New York *Times* reviewer thought *The Miracle Man* the only 1919 film worthy to stand beside *Broken Blossoms*, and Hazel Simpson Naylor, in *Motion Picture*, concluded her notice by observing, somewhat incoherently, that "the nearest approach to any rival of Mr. Griffith for screenic honors falls to Mr. Tucker." As usual it was Johnson who said it best: "As a study of genuine human beings, as an exhibition of the instinctive triumph of the better nature when the better nature has a chance, as a perfect fabric of life as it is lived—alternately as funny as a Chaplin and pathetic as a [David] Warfield scene—and as an adroitly constructed drama, rising from climax to climax and never missing a telling point, I do not recall that the silversheet has ever offered anything any better than this, and few pieces as good." And, in conclusion: "Upon this enterprise, George Loane Tucker steps into that small but dazzling arena where only the sunshine masters stand." These judgments did not seem extravagant to me at the time, and I regret that, since only a small portion of *The Miracle Man* has survived, I cannot now check up on my original impression.

Tucker never pulled his punches in showing what his sinners needed to be redeemed from. There was no glossing over either the nastiness or the lure of sin; it was in this film, not in *Traffic in Souls*, that Tucker made us feel the power of sex. Yet sexual sin was not the worst of their transgressions any more than it is the worst of sins in Dante's *Divine Comedy* or in Dante's theological master, St. Thomas Aquinas.

Again, though there is considerable testimony available to attest the possibility of some of the Patriarch's cures, it would be a mistake to judge the picture by what one may believe about such things. The real miracle lies elsewhere, in the appeal that sheer human goodness makes to the buried seed of goodness in those who have done their best to kill it—the "Lord's mark" on every human creature, as *Huckleberry Finn* expresses it, or what Browning calls that which a man may waste or desecrate but never quite lose. It may be hard to believe that the whole quartette could have been redeemed. Perhaps too the "Dope's" story may seem to have been developed less than the others, or perhaps he only interests us less. But such considerations do not greatly weaken the dramatic impact of the film.

It has been said that Thomas Meighan could not manage the scene in which, under the workings of Divine Grace, he dissolves in tears, and that Tucker, to get the effect he wanted, was obliged to work upon his emotions as a man, whereupon the tears began to flow so copiously that they would not stop. If this is true, the effect shown on the screen was, in this instance, nature, not art, which involves an interesting commentary on the difference between one aspect of acting on the screen and on the stage, where the desirable effect that may have been achieved accidentally at 9:20 tonight must be recreated at 9:20 every night and at 3:20 on matinees. (*E. W.*)

Above: *The Frog.* Below: *The gang: Tom Burke, the Frog, the Dope, and Rose.*

Above: *The Patriarch with Rose, after her reformation.* Below: *Rose and Tom Burke.*

EYES OF YOUTH

An Equity production. Released October 26, 1919. 7 reels.

Producer: Harry Garson. Director: Albert Parker. Screenplay: Charles Everard Whittaker (based on the stage play by Max Marcin and Charles Guernon). Photography: Arthur Edeson.

CAST: Clara Kimball Young (*Gina Ashling*); Gareth Hughes (*Her Brother*); Pauline Starke (*Her Sister*); Sam Sothern (*Her Father*); Edmund Lowe (*Her Suitor*); Ralph Lewis (*Another*); Milton Sills (*Still Another*); Vincent Serrano (*The Yogi*); Rudolph Valentino (*A Professional Corespondent*); William Courtleigh; E. M. Kimball.

SYNOPSIS: Gina Ashling has a voice of operatic calibre, but her family urges that it is her duty to remain with them and contribute to their support instead of going to Paris to study. A wise man from the East shows her in his crystal what her life will be if she follows the Path of Duty as a tired and unappreciated schoolteacher, the Path of Ambition as a singer, or the Path of Wealth, as the wife of the man her father wishes her to marry. All end in misery, disgrace, and/or disintegration of character. To save her soul Gina decides to marry the man she loves.

COMMENTARY: Clara Kimball Young (1890–1960) may not have been one of the great artists of motion-picture history, but she certainly played an important part in its development. Not only did she enjoy tremendous popularity; she was one of the first stars to form her own production company, and far-ranging changes in booking practices followed.

Then the wife of James Young, actor and director, she began with Vitagraph in 1912, appearing first as Anne Boleyn in the one-reel *Cardinal Wolsey*. At this time she was a dark, svelte, lissome girl, with amazingly large and beautiful eyes. In 1914 she finished second in *The Motion Picture Magazine* popularity contest; Earle Williams, another Vitagrapher, was first, and Mary Pickford came in third. Mrs. Young made many films for Vitagraph, mostly one-reelers, and she continued into their feature era, appearing in *The Little Minister* and in *My Official Wife*.

In 1915 she became the mainstay of the new World Film Company, being seen, for instance, in *The Reason Why, Camille,* and *Trilby,* which last was directed by Maurice Tourneur. From 1917 to 1919 her films were handled by Lewis J. Selznick's Select Company; these included *The Common Law, The Easiest Way, The Price She Paid, Magda, The Marionettes,* and others, films of widely varying literary inspiration but mostly pretty daring stuff for the time. By now she was more matronly than girlish-looking (she was also elaborately and expensively gowned), and her following seems largely to have been made up of housewives, middle-aged and over, who no doubt found it easier to identify with her (or aspire to be like her) than to stand in such relationships to the younger actresses then in vogue. She must indeed have been an important element in drawing this important segment of the population into the film theaters. Later she appeared for Equity and Metro,

Gina's brother, Gina's father, the Yogi, a suitor (Ralph Lewis), Gina, her sister; at the window, far right, the actors Milton Sills (as another suitor) and William Courtleigh.

but she did not manage her later career skillfully, and her stardom ended in 1925, though she was seen in a supporting role as late as 1938.

Eyes of Youth, which had served Marjorie Rambeau on the stage, is not necessarily Clara Kimball Young's best film, but it gives her wider scope than most of her pictures did, though it cannot be said that she took full advantage of all of them. She seems lethargic, almost cataleptic, in the "Path of Duty" portion and "makes up" for this, as the saying goes, by overacting in "The Path of Ambition," but this is not, or not wholly, her fault, for the conception of an opera singer's life presented in this film seems indistinguishable from that which used to appear in yellowbacks intended for the servant's hall. Her best work comes at the very end, as the drug-sodden derelict, desolate on a city street in winter, at the end of "The Path of Wealth," which is quite impressively done.

There is more hocus-pocus than mystical insight in the Wise Man of the East framework imposed upon this film. Nor is it possible to believe that any one woman could possibly have all the potentialities explored here; if this is true, then human beings have no character but are merely the sports of circumstance. But such speculations take *Eyes of Youth* much too seriously.

As the credits show, the film boasted a remarkable cast of veterans and young actors whose careers were on the upswing. Rudolph Valentino, his career all before him, made a brief appearance as a slimy little underworld rat; when the picture was reissued at the height of his later vogue, he was billed as its "star"! (*E. W.*)

Above: *Gina and the professional corespondent. (Rudolph Valentino here had one of his first featured roles.)* Below: *The performers include (left to right) Valentino, Clara Kimball Young, Ralph Lewis, Milton Sills, and E. M. Kimball.*

ANNE OF GREEN GABLES

A Realart production. Released by Paramount, November 23, 1919. 7 reels.

Director: William Desmond Taylor. Screenplay: Frances Marion (based on the novel by L. M. Montgomery). Photography: Hal Young.

(*Anne of Green Gables* was remade in 1934 by RKO, with Anne Shirley in the title role.)

CAST: Mary Miles Minter (*Anne Shirley*); George Stewart (*Gilbert Blythe*); Marcia Harris (*Marilla Cuthbert*); Frederick Burton (*Matthew Cuthbert*); E. T. Chailles (*Abdenage Pie*); Leila Romer (*Mrs. Pie*); Lincoln Stedman (*Jumbo Pie*); Hazel Sexton (*Josie Pie*); Master Russell Hewitt (*Anthony Pie*); Albert Hackett (*Robert*); Maurice Lovelle (*Diana Barry*); Mrs. Caroline Lee (*Mrs. Barry*); Jack B. Hollis (*Rev. Figtree*).

SYNOPSIS: Anne Shirley, an orphan, is adopted by Matthew Cuthbert and his spinster sister Marilla. Since they had expected a boy, they are at first disappointed, but they come to love her dearly. The film concerns her adventures and misadventures with friends and enemies (notably the Pies) and her growing up at the Cuthbert home, Green Gables. Highlights include her selling a neighbor's cow by mistake, pummeling a boy who had dropped an apple on her head, just as Marilla is singing her praises to the minister, and breaking up a picnic by caressing a skunk which she has mistaken for a cat.

COMMENTARY: Mary Miles Minter won fame in childhood when her acting in *The Littlest Rebel,* with Dustin and William Farnum, created a stage legend. She was on the screen from 1912, but few of her early vehicles, with Metro and American, were memorable. In 1919 she went to Zukor, who released her pictures first under the Realart banner and then as Paramounts. Though these films were not all equally good, they were, in general, much better than what American had been giving her and offered far better acting opportunities.

Anne of Green Gables was the first, and though it did not present her with a difficult role, it did provide as delightful and effective a showcase for her personality as she was ever to find. Stories about girls' growing up were very popular early in the century, and though Kate Douglas Wiggin's *Rebecca of Sunnybrook Farm* was never equaled in kind by any other writer, both Eleanor H. Porter's *Pollyanna* and *Anne of Green Gables* by the Canadian writer L. M. Montgomery proved popular enough to spawn many sequels.

From another point of view, *Anne* was less fortunate for Miss Minter. It was the first of four pictures directed for

her by William Desmond Taylor. On February 1, 1922, Taylor died in a murder mystery that has never been solved, and Miss Minter was indiscreet enough to proclaim that she had been in love with him and that he had loved her. Though no scintilla of evidence reflecting adversely upon her character was ever brought forth, the newspapers and the scandalmongers slaughtered her, and when her contract ran out, Paramount pusillanimously failed to renew it. It was the heyday of the "Hollywood scandals," and the industry was panic-ridden. *The Trail of the Lonesome Pine* (1923) was Miss Minter's last film. A career that had begun with such brilliance was cruelly aborted when she was 21. (*E. W.*)

Above: *Anne breaks up the picnic party: she holds Jumbo Pie, while Robert looks disgusted in the background. (Albert Hackett, who played Robert, was later to become a prominent screenwriter.)*
Below: *Anne's show of affection for another outrages her sweetheart, Gilbert Blythe.*

MALE AND FEMALE

A Famous Players-Lasky production. Released by Paramount Pictures, November 30, 1919. 9 reels.

Producer and Director: Cecil B. DeMille. Screenplay: Jeanie Macpherson (based on the play *The Admirable Crichton*, by J. M. Barrie). Photography: Alvin Wyckoff. Film Editor: Anne Bauchens. Art Director: Wilfred Buckland. Costumes: Mitchell Leisen.

(*The Admirable Crichton* was first filmed in England in 1918 by G. B. Samuelson. A second British version was produced in 1956 and released in the U.S. by Columbia as *Paradise Lagoon*.)

CAST: Gloria Swanson (*Lady Mary Lasenby*); Thomas Meighan (*Crichton, the Butler*); Lila Lee (*Tweeny*); Theodore Roberts (*Lord Loam*); Raymond Hatton (*Hon. Ernest Wolley*); Mildred Reardon (*Agatha Lasenby*); Bebe Daniels (*The King's Favorite*); Robert Cain (*Lord Brocklehurst*); Julia Faye (*Susan*); Rhy Darby (*Lady Eileen Dun Craigie*); Mayme Kelso (*Lady Brocklehurst*); Edmund Burns (*Treherne*); Henry Woodward (*McGuire*); Sydney Deane (*Thomas*); Wesley Barry ("*Buttons*"); Edna Mae Cooper (*Fisher*); Lillian Leighton (*Mrs. Perkins*); Guy Oliver (*Pilot of Lord Loam's Yacht*); Clarence Burton (*Yacht Captain*).

SYNOPSIS: When Lord Loam's yacht is wrecked, those on board include Lady Mary Lasenby; her fiancé, Lord Brocklehurst, whom she does not really love; the butler, Crichton; and the scullery maid, Tweeny, who adores him. On the island where they now find themselves, the only question is survival, and the class distinctions that had separated people in England disappear. Crichton reveals himself a very able man and Lord Brocklehurst a nonentity, while Lady Mary is amazed to find herself not only taking orders from Crichton and performing tasks she never thought of doing before but actually coming to love him. After the party has been rescued, however, they all soon settle back into their old ways. Lady Mary goes ahead with her plan to marry Lord Brocklehurst, and Tweeny becomes Crichton's bride.

COMMENTARY: "Although the world is topsy-turvy," wrote S. J. Perelman in 1952, "DeMille still remains the same. His latest pictures display the same baroque pomp, the same good old five-cent philosophy, and the same lofty disregard for sense. *Male and Female* could be remade today with equal success at the box office." What Perelman neglected to point out was that DeMille's basic ingredients might not change, but the director's artistry did. There is far more artistic endeavor, far more directorial skills and ingenuity visible, in a DeMille production such as *Male and Female* than may be seen in his later monolithic bores such as *The Greatest Show on Earth* or *The Ten Commandments* of 1956.

In a way, *Male and Female* represents the highest level the director-producer attained, not only so far as the art of the cinema is concerned, but also in terms of understanding exactly what an audience wanted and expected from a visit to the cinema, and giving them just that and nothing more. DeMille took J. M. Barrie's play *The Admirable Crichton*, removed all of its whimsy and much of its satire and humor, and in their place substituted sex and sophisti-

A bored socialite and an equally bored maid: Lady Mary and Tweeny.

cation—or, to be more precise, what passed for sex and sophistication in 1919. Gloria Swanson's bedroom is prominently featured in the opening scenes, and Miss Swanson—whom one critic described as "the glorious exponent of sex incarnate"—is also required to take a bath in a scene that is possibly the most famous moment in any DeMille production. Nor does DeMille let the story's contemporary setting prevent his introducing an historical tableau, with Thomas Meighan as a Babylonian King and Bebe Daniels appearing all too fleetingly as a court favorite.

Cecil B. DeMille had been working his way toward a film such as *Male and Female* through the teens; it is no exaggeration to say that *The Cheat, Old Wives for New* and *Don't Change Your Husband*, in particular, were immediate antecedents to *Male and Female*. They were all concerned with male/female relationships and all hinted at sexual infidelity. With *Male and Female*, DeMille reached his zenith in this area. The Twenties features that followed, such as *The Ten Commandments, Manslaughter, The Road to Yesterday*, and even *King of Kings*, might have more spectacle, but they most certainly did not reveal any new cinematic techniques—the parting of the Red Sea aside—and most certainly could not pander more to the baser needs of the audience.

There was almost a cold precision to the way in which DeMille, usually in partnership with Jeanie Macpherson, conceived and produced his films. Julian Johnson, writing in the December, 1919, issue of *Photoplay*, hit the nail on the head when he commented, "It is a typical DeMille production—audacious, glittering, intriguing, superlatively elegant and quite without heart. It reminds me of one of our great California flowers, glowing with all the colors of the rainbow and devoid of fragrance." (*A. S.*)

Above: *Lord Brocklehurst, Ernest Wolley, Crichton, and Lord Loam. Below: Tweeny and Crichton.*
("Here Miss Lee realizes, for the first time," commented Julian Johnson in the December, 1919
"Photoplay," "the cinemic dream that Mr. Lasky had when he espied her shrouded in vaudeville.")

Above: *Lady Mary.* (MALE AND FEMALE *provided Cecil B. DeMille with an opportunity to have Gloria Swanson display more flesh than was usually shown by actresses of the period.)* Below: *Crichton as King, with his favorite, in the historical sequence: "I was a King in Babylon and you were a Christian slave."*

Above: *The admirable Crichton and his devoted slavey, Tweeny.* Below: *"Humanity is assuredly growing cleaner—but is it growing more artistic? Women bathe more often, but not as beautifully as did their ancient Sisters. Why shouldn't the Bath Room express as much Art and Beauty as the Drawing Room?"*

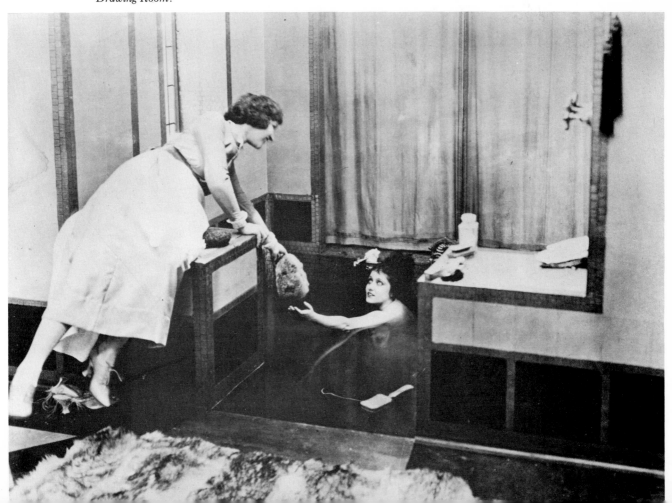

BEHIND THE DOOR

A Thomas H. Ince production. Released by Paramount-Artcraft, January, 1920. 7 reels.

Producer: Thomas H. Ince. Director: Irvin Willat. Screenplay: Luther A. Reed (based on the *Collier's Weekly* story by Gouverneur Morris). Photography: Frank M. Blount.

CAST: Hobart Bosworth (*Oscar Krug*); Jane Novak (*Alice Morse*); Wallace Beery (*Lieutenant Brandt*); James Gordon (*Bill Tavish*); Dick Wain (*McQuestion*); J. P. Lockney (*Matthew Morse*); Gibson Gowland (*Gideon Blank*); Otto Hoffman (*Mark Arnold*).

SYNOPSIS: Captain Oscar Krug, a taxidermist of German descent, lives in a small seacoast town in Maine, and because of his ancestry is attacked by the locals at America's entry into the First World War. Loyal to his country, he fights a hand-to-hand battle with his detractors and wins their respect. Krug enlists in the navy, and his new, young wife succeeds in boarding his ship, which is sunk by a German submarine. Only Krug and his wife survive, and after days on the open sea in a small boat are spotted by a German submarine, the brutal captain of which takes the wife aboard and leaves Krug to perish. Later, Krug is rescued, and in time sinks the submarine and takes its captain prisoner. After wining and dining the captain, Krug learns of his wife's rape and death, and takes his revenge by skinning the captain alive.

COMMENTARY: It is doubtful the silent American cinema produced a film in worse taste or as sadistic as *Behind the Door*, which Frederick James Smith in *Motion Picture Classic* (March, 1920) described as "an opus in brutality—an intermezzo in gory revenge." As anti-German propaganda, the film has no equal. Its bloody, melodramatic plot has never been bettered. Which film of recent years could boast a story in which a young wife is savagely raped by a bestial submarine captain and his equally villainous crew, and then, when all are through with her, is dispatched from the vessel by way of the torpedo gun? Aside from the 1934 production of *The Black Cat*, where else can one find an ending in which the villain is tied up and almost skinned alive? I say almost, for the villain dies before the ordeal is through, prompting the taxidermist hero to sigh, "I swore I would skin him alive, but he died on me—damn him!"

Why Thomas Ince should have chosen to produce such a classic piece of anti-German propaganda more than a year after the signing of the Armistice is unexplained. It certainly did not disturb contemporary reviewers, who were full of admiration for the production, with one critic comparing it to the sombre tales of Edgar Allan Poe.

Behind the Door marked the return to the screen, after an absence of a couple of years, of Hobart Bosworth, a dignified performer who was out of place in such a bloodthirsty piece. "Power with geniality" was a phrase used by one writer which admirably describes Bosworth, who, after *Behind the Door*, seemed fated for a while to appear in nothing but sea pictures, following it with *Below the Surface* and *The Sea Wolf,* both produced in 1920 by Ince. As his wife in the film, Jane Novak achieved screen stardom. She was a talented actress (perhaps at her best opposite Buck Jones in Frank Borzage's *Lazybones* of 1925) who has been for too long neglected by today's film historians. (*A. S.*)

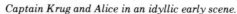
Captain Krug and Alice in an idyllic early scene.

Above: *The brutal fight sequence in which Krug proves his Americanism to the townspeople.* Below: *Captain Krug's wife, "outraged beyond the power of words to express it," as one reviewer described the sequence in which she is gang-raped by the crew of the German submarine.*

Above: *Krug takes Lieutenant Brandt "behind the door," and prepares to skin him alive.* Below: *Krug: "I swore I would skin him alive, but he died on me—damn him!"*

DR. JEKYLL AND MR. HYDE

A Famous Players-Lasky production. Released by Paramount-Artcraft, April, 1920. 7 reels (6,355 ft.).

Director: John S. Robertson. Screenplay: Clara S. Beranger (based on the story by Robert Louis Stevenson). Photography: Roy F. Overbaugh.

(Robert Louis Stevenson's novel has been filmed many times: in 1908 by Selig, in 1909 by Nordisk, in 1912 by Thanhouser, in 1913 by Imp, in 1920 by Pioneer, in 1931 by Paramount, in 1941 by MGM, etc.)

CAST: John Barrymore (*Dr. Jekyll/Mr. Hyde*); Martha Mansfield (*Millicent Carew*); Brandon Hurst (*Sir George Carew*); Charles Lane (*Dr. Richard Lanyon*); J. Malcolm Dunn (*John Utterson*); Cecil Clovelly (*Edward Enfield*); Nita Naldi (*Gina*); George Stevens (*Poole*); Louis Wolheim (*Master of Ceremonies in Dive*).

SYNOPSIS: Dr. Henry Jekyll, the Saint Anthony of London, maintains a clinic for the poor at his own expense. Unorthodox and experimental in medicine, Jekyll is absorbed in psychological experiments. When tempted by his fiancée's father, Sir George Carew, who taunts him with being afraid of temptation, he concocts a drug that enables him to separate man's lower nature from his nobility. Thereupon, in his Edward Hyde aspect, he sets out upon a career of indulgence in the underworld. As Jekyll he had repelled the advances of the dancer Gina in the dive to which Carew had conducted him; as Hyde, he returns to her, makes her his mistress, ruins her, and casts her off. He kills a little boy by tramping on him. By the time conscience awakens, it is too late to turn back, for he has now begun to turn into Hyde without the drug. When Carew discovers his secret, Jekyll/Hyde kills him. Confined to his laboratory, with the law closing in upon him, he poisons himself out of an old Italian poison ring he had filched from Gina.

COMMENTARY: Robert Louis Stevenson's *Strange Case of Dr. Jekyll and Mr. Hyde* was first written as a "shocker," then recharactered as an ethical parable upon the insistence of the author's wife. It was one of the earliest studies of dual personality in literature and is still the most famous.

Richard Mansfield had Thomas Russell Sullivan turn it into a play for him, which he first acted at the Boston Museum on May 9, 1887, and retained to the end of his life. Mansfield went through two transformation scenes on stage—from Hyde to Jekyll in Act III and from Jekyll to Hyde in Act IV—using lights but no makeup. Barrymore changes from Jekyll to Hyde five times (all but the first without the drug) and from Hyde to Jekyll twice, the second time after death.

John Barrymore first revealed his capacity as a serious actor in Arthur Hopkins' stage production of Galsworthy's *Justice* in 1916. In 1920, the year of our film, which was John S. Robertson's first important production, he appeared on Broadway as Richard III, using makeup suggestive of, but much less horrific than, what he employs as Hyde. Robertson went on to realize his full potential as a director (he died at 86 in 1964), but Barrymore, who in 1920 seemed to stand on the threshold of one of the

Sir George Carew tempts Dr. Jekyll.

greatest careers in the history of the American theater, did not have the stability necessary to develop and maintain it consistently.

In Stevenson's story, a man named Sir Danvers Carew is murdered by Hyde but has no contact with Dr. Jekyll. Sullivan made Carew the blameless father of Jekyll's fiancée Agnes and had Hyde kill him in Act I. The film rechristens Agnes as Millicent and, borrowing a motive and some language from Oscar Wilde's *The Picture of Dorian Gray*, makes her father Jekyll's tempter and evil genius. If it was Sullivan who introduced a love interest into the tale, it was the makers of this film who developed Hyde's adventures in an underworld filled with gloomy settings and peopled by fantastic types of ugliness and depravity, suggestive of the German films that were popular in America at the time. The sexual element introduced here in connection with Gina did not go undeveloped in later *Jekyll and Hyde* films.

"The Great Profile" and the nobility of spirit its possessor could still command in 1920 are much in evidence, but it is Hyde's Grand Guignol bestiality in which Barrymore seems to revel. Though much of this is horror for horror's sake, the film still seems to the present writer superior to what we were to receive later in the productions starring Fredric March and Spencer Tracy.

The appearance of Martha Mansfield as Millicent adds a melancholy interest to the film and horror of a different variety from Edward Hyde's. Three years later, while making a new version of *The Warrens of Virginia*, she was burned to death when somebody dropped a lighted match upon the crinoline type of dress she was wearing. (*E. W.*)

Above: *Dr. Jekyll, with Dr. Lanyon, who has no sympathy with his experiments.* Below: *Mr. Hyde, with the master of ceremonies in the dive where he meets Gina.*

TREASURE ISLAND

An Artcraft production. Released by Paramount, April, 1920. 5 reels (5,134 ft.).

Director: Maurice Tourneur. Screenplay: Stephen Fox (based on the novel by Robert Louis Stevenson). Photography: René Guissart.

(*Treasure Island* has been filmed at least four other times: in 1917 by Fox, in 1934 by MGM, in 1950 by Walt Disney, and in 1972 by National General.)

CAST: Shirley Mason (*Jim Hawkins*); Josie Melville (*Mrs. Hawkins*); Al Filson (*Bill Bones*); Wilton Taylor (*Black Dog*); Lon Chaney (*Pew/Merry*); Charles Ogle (*Long John Silver*); Joseph Singleton (*Israel Hands*); Bull Montana (*Morgan*); Harry Holden (*Captain Smollett*); Sydney Dean (*Squire Trelawney*); Charles Hill Mailes (*Dr. Livesey*).

SYNOPSIS: "On the whole," wrote Adele Whitely Fletcher, "Maurice Tourneur doesn't take Stevenson's *Treasure Island* nearly as seriously as did Stevenson. He gives it to the silversheet with less of the adventure with which the printed word endowed it and more of the whimsy. Generally, it runs true to the story with combination of incidents now and then and at times a deviation which was evidently done for a better continuity in the necessary length." Perhaps the most striking addition was to have Billy Bones stabbed to death by old blind Pew instead of being merely frightened into his death by him. But the essential outline of the tale remained.

COMMENTARY: "Shirley Mason's only shortcoming in the character of Jim Hawkins," wrote Edward Weitzel in his review of *Treasure Island* in *The Moving Picture World*, "is due to her inability to conceal her sex." But "shortcoming," surely, is one of the most exquisitely ill-chosen words in criticism. Who in the world could possibly have wanted her to?

Maurice Tourneur had the richest aesthetic background of any early film director. In France he had been associated with both Rodin and Puvis de Chavannes. As a teenager he had tried his hand at magazine and book illustration and designed posters and fabrics, and, according to George Geltzer, had even worked on Puvis de Chavannes's sketches for the famous murals over the grand staircase in the Boston Public Library. If he didn't, he obviously ought to have done so! Nobody who knows the work of this exquisite painter can fail to discern a resemblance between his paintings and Tourneur's films.

The casting of Shirley Mason, then, strikes the keynote for the understanding of the director's approach to *Treasure Island*. It meant that he would *not* turn out the kind of film that Jackie Cooper and Wallace Beery made for MGM in 1934. For Jim Hawkins is neither an idealized essence of childhood like Oliver Twist nor a fairy child like Peter Pan. He is a real boy. If he was to be played by a girl, all else must be in tune and all other values yield to pictorialism. And so they did.

Mutiny on the "Hispaniola."

On first consideration, the changes that Tourneur made in the story might seem to militate against this purpose—the fearsomeness of the pirates, the killing of Bones by Pew. Actually this will not hold, for the pirates are not realistically conceived; their affinity lies with the fearsome kind of creatures that children conjure up to scare themselves stiff with on Hallowe'en. Even Edward Weitzel, who found that "the few added incidents are full of drama," went on to observe that "the one feature of the production that can be called in question is the cave where the pirate's treasure is found, with the bewildering display of gold pieces on the floor. Only Aladdin and the wonderful lamp could have created either the cave or the gold." But he did not stop there. "However, *Treasure Island* is a first cousin to all the stories in the Arabian Nights, and no one is going to begrudge Jim the size of his treasure and his joy at the thought of how he can lavish it on his mother."

If *Treasure Island* was not quite so good a film as *A Poor Little Rich Girl*, *The Blue Bird*, or *Prunella*, the reason is that this time the director was not handed material that *in itself* was completely in tune with his own mind and temperament and ideally suited to his needs. For that very reason, however, it provides the interest of showing how materials that, albeit romantic, had been differently conceived and devised, could be recharacterized and adapted by him. Maurice Tourneur was a sufficiently great artist to be allowed this privilege. (*E. W.*)

Above: *Jim and Long John Silver, with the pirates.* Below: *Jim corners a pirate.*

REMODELING HER HUSBAND

A New Art Film Company production. Released by Paramount-Artcraft, June, 1920. 5 reels (4,844 ft.).

Director: Lillian Gish. Story and Screenplay: Dorothy Elizabeth Carter. Photography: George W. Hill.

CAST: Dorothy Gish (*Janie Wakefield*); James Rennie (*Jack Valentine*); Marie Burke (*Mrs. Wakefield*); Downing Clarke (*Mr. Wakefield*); Frank Kingdom (*Mr. Valentine*).

SYNOPSIS: Vivacious Janie Wakefield marries Jack Valentine, despite his roving eye. His weakness for a pretty face causes endless trouble until Janie leaves him, goes into business for herself, and makes him realize that she is such a wonderful wife that he should become a submissive and repentant husband.

COMMENTARY: It is one of the frustrations of studying early film history that so many intriguing productions are no longer extant. Nowhere is this frustration more keenly felt than as it applies to Lillian Gish's only effort as a director, *Remodeling Her Husband.*

The story behind the making of the film has already been told by Miss Gish in her autobiography and elsewhere, but it is worth summarizing here. D. W. Griffith had almost completed his Mamaroneck studios, and while he was shooting in Florida, he suggested to Lillian that she direct a film starring her sister. Lillian selected the story, designed the scenery, hired the technical crew, handled a tricky situation of shooting in New York City streets without a permit by befriending a policeman enamoured of her performance in *Broken Blossoms,* and, the biggest chore of all, managed to get Griffith's studio in operation ready for his return. The film cost $58,000 to produce, and, according to its director, earned back more than ten times that amount. Lillian recalled for me, "When Griffith came back, I asked him why he did that to me, had me get a studio ready and make a picture when it was my first one and such an awful chore. He said, 'Because I needed my studio built quickly. I knew they'd work faster for a girl than they would for me. I'm no fool.'"

None of the contemporary critics cared for the story line, but they were unanimous in their praise for Miss Gish's directorial abilities. "Lillian Gish has gone back to acting," wrote Burns Mantle in *Photoplay* (September, 1920), "but we'd like to tell her that she is almost as good a directress as she is an actress—and that's going some." Commented Frederick James Smith in *Motion Picture Classic* (October, 1920), "After observing Dorothy Gish's *Remodeling Her Husband,* we are confident that Lillian Gish could easily develop into a director of fine originality." Laurence Reid wrote in *Motion Picture News* (June 19, 1920), "Lillian Gish shows her versatility as the director and her ability to make the most of the story is a creditable achievement."

Remodeling Her Husband could easily prove to be a feminist's delight, for as Burns Mantle commented in *Photoplay,* "This is a woman's picture. A woman wrote it, a woman stars in it, a woman was its director. And women will enjoy it most. It does an unusual and daring thing; it presents the feminine point of view in plot, in captions, in sets and acting."

If for no other reason than to prove that there were capable women behind the camera in the silent era, one wishes that *Remodeling Her Husband* might be rediscovered. Hopefully, it would counteract the overemotional, undeserved zeal with which Dorothy Arzner's works have been praised, and illustrate that a great actress such as Lillian Gish could also be perhaps not a great, but at least a highly competent director. (*A. S.*)

Janie succeeds in gaining Jack's attention. (Dorothy Gish was already a prominent Paramount comedy star, whereas James Rennie was making his screen debut.)

Above: *A misunderstanding between Jack and Janie. (Within months of making the picture, Dorothy Gish and James Rennie married in real life.)* Below: *Mrs. Wakefield, Mr. Wakefield, Janie, and Jack.*

SUDS

Director: Jack Dillon. Screenplay: Waldemar Young (based on the stage play *'Op o' Me Thumb,* by Frederick Fenn and Richard Bryce). Photography: Charles Rosher.

CAST: Mary Pickford (*Amanda Afflick*); Albert Austin (*Horace Greensmith*); Harold Goodwin (*Benjamin Pillsbury Jones*); Madame Rose Dione (*Madame Jeanne Gallifilet Didier*); Lavender (*The Horse*).

SYNOPSIS: Romantically inclined Amanda Afflick is a London laundry worker who weaves a tale around a shirt left at the laundry eight months previous by Horace Greensmith. She tells the other girls that the shirt is the property of her fiancé, that she is really the daughter of a duke, and that her lover will return to claim both her and his shirt. Ben Jones, the laundry's driver, is in love with Amanda, but her thoughts are only of Horace Greensmith. When Lavender, the old laundry horse, is to be sent to the glue factory, Amanda sacrifices her savings to buy him. After Lavender has been removed from Amanda's room by the angry tenants below, Lady Burke, a philanthropist, visits the slums and agrees to have the horse taken to her country estate. In the meantime, Horace Greensmith returns for his shirt, and Amanda tearfully persuades him to pretend to the other girls in the laundry that he is her lover, but then he departs. As he leaves, Amanda cries to herself, while Ben Jones stands sadly outside staring at the flowers he has brought for her. An alternate, happy ending has Amanda and Ben together with Lavender on Lady Burke's estate.

COMMENTARY: Mary Pickford completed *Suds* just before marrying Douglas Fairbanks on March 28, 1920 and starting off to Europe on their honeymoon. It was based on a play that Maude Adams had done on the New York stage in 1905, when the critics had praised her for having the courage to "make herself so pitiably unattractive, with anaemic skin, shuffling gait, scrawny figure and thin hair." Her characterization of the hapless slavey was called one of the most attractive things she had ever done. "It was the acme of genuine pathos, a most moving and telling portrayal of unhappy girlhood."

Mary's production, one fears, was less appreciated by either press or public. Adele Whitely Fletcher, to be sure, beat the drums for it in *Motion Picture Magazine:* "Mary's little Amanda is very real. We doubt if we will ever forget her and it has probably taught us to be more understanding of any little Amandas we know—to think more about their right to dream." But even she wanted another *Poor Little Rich Girl, Rebecca,* or *Pollyanna* next time round, and her colleague on *Motion Picture Classic,* Frederick James Smith, who described *Suds* as "a drab tragedy, told largely in terms of Keystone comedy," admitted that it left him "rather cold." Burns Mantle in *Photoplay* found it "not particularly good entertainment. The pathos, for one thing, is laid on a bit thick, forcing the suggestion of unreality. It is all artistically screened and beautifully pictured; the dream of a little laundry girl, who sees in the clouds of suds that rise from her tub visions of the grand young gentleman who is one day to raise her from her lowly estate, is amusingly set in the tone of the story, and the broader comedy incidents of Amanda's turning her room over to Lavender, the poor old delivery horse she saved from the glue factory, delight the children. But *Suds* is an effort to compromise between the real and the unreal, and to me such compromises are never entirely successful."

Laurence Reid, in *Motion Picture News,* called Amanda "a vest pocket edition of Unity [in *Stella Maris*], without one-half the color and vitality." Perhaps that was the trouble. Amanda even looked like Unity, and, as Geraldine Farrar used to say when her audiences begged her to repeat a song, the second cream puff never tastes as good as the first. Having proved that she could do it with Unity, Mary did not really need to do it again. Moreover, *Stella Maris* had given us an Amanda without robbing us of "Our Mary" in the person of Stella herself, while *Suds* had only a glimpse of the popular Mary in the dream fantasy sequence in which Amanda saw herself gorgeously gowned and inhabiting a palace.

These reactions, if I have described them rightly, are all quite understandable. They were nevertheless also quite wrong. Obviously *Suds* was very special fare, and obviously no Pickford fan would have wanted Mary to confine herself to a succession of films in kind. Nevertheless it was a brilliant film in its own right, abundantly able to stand on its own feet, without reference to either *Stella* or Mary's usual product. It was a fine eccentric comedy, as subtly blended with pathos as Chaplin himself could have achieved. It is simply incredible that the so often acute aficionados of silent screen comedy should have ignored it as they have. Even Walter Kerr fails to mention it in his top-flight book on *The Silent Clowns.* (E. W.)

Above: *A beautiful, and somewhat idealized, photograph of Amanda by James Abbe.*
Below: *Amanda as she sees herself in fantasy.*

Above: *Amanda with Lavender.* Below: *When Horace Greensmith returned.*

WHILE NEW YORK SLEEPS

A William Fox production. Released August, 1920. 8 reels.

Director: Charles J. Brabin. Screenplay: Charles J. Brabin and Thomas F. Fallon. Photography: George W. Lane.

(In 1921, Universal released a one-reel Star Comedy titled *While New York Snores.*)

CAST:

A Story of the Suburbs
Estelle Taylor (*A Wife*); William Locke (*Her Husband*); Marc MacDermott (*A Strange Visitor*); Harry Sothern (*A Burglar*).

The Gay White Way
Estelle Taylor (*The Vamp*); Marc MacDermott (*The Man*); Harry Sothern (*The—er—Friend*).

A Tragedy of the East Side
Marc MacDermott (*The Paralytic* [*Peter*]); Harry Sothern (*His Son* [*Ned*]); Estelle Taylor (*The Girl* [*Nina*]); Earl Metcalf (*The Gangster* [*Buck Slade*]).

SYNOPSIS:

A Story of the Suburbs

While her husband is attending a business meeting and the servants are out, a wealthy suburbanite is visited by her former husband, who she believes died four years previously. He threatens to tell her husband of his existence unless provided with money. After he leaves and she retires, a burglar breaks in, but is forced to hide when the former husband reappears in a drunken state and attacks the wife. When the two discover the burglar, he shoots the former husband just as husband No. 2 returns. The wife helps the burglar escape and tells her husband that she shot, in self-defense, the man who to all appearances was the burglar.

The Gay White Way

When a victim whom the Vamp has seduced and who had set her up in an apartment, is threatened with divorce by his wife, he tells the Vamp he must leave her. She and an accomplice trick the man into believing she has killed herself because of him and into paying blackmail money. However, the victim proves to be a detective and the couple are arrested. As a final twist, the Vamp and the detective are seen in old age as a happily married couple.

A Tragedy of the East Side

Nina marries Ned, not because she loves him, but for convenience' sake. When thieves break into the warehouse where Ned is night watchman, he is able to call the police and all but one of the gang are captured. The one who escapes, Buck Slade, accidentally comes to Ned's home, where Nina is attracted to him and hides him. The only person who is aware of what is going on is Ned's paralytic father, who can only hear and see. With his eyes, the father conveys to Ned what is happening, and as a result Ned is killed by the gangster. When the police arrive to tell Nina of her husband's death, the father again uses his eyes to tell the police where Buck is, and the father has the satisfaction of seeing both Buck and Nina die.

COMMENTARY: "To the countless millions of friends known and unknown in all quarters of the globe, to those who built her skyscrapers, her giant industries, to those who toil in her streets, to those who have known her prosperity, misery, heartaches and peace, we dedicate with just pride this chronicle of the great Metropolis, New York."

Thus reads the opening title to *While New York Sleeps,* one of the best films of 1920 and one of the finest films ever produced to be set in New York City. Its three stories illustrate different aspects of New York life, from the gaiety and glamor of its nightlife to the seeming tranquility of suburban living and the poverty and misery of its East Side inhabitants. Coincidentally, the film provided unique glimpses of the East River and two New York landmarks of the period, the Ziegfeld Frolic and the Palais Royal, with the girls at the former demonstrating the new dance craze of the Shimmy.

All three stories are very much in the style of O. Henry. The first two, which make up the first half of the picture, are cleverly contrived, with "A Story of the Suburbs" allowing for a considerable amount of emoting by Estelle Taylor, a dramatic silent star whose best work was probably in King Vidor's production of *Street Scene.* It is the third story, "A Tragedy of the East Side," that dominates the film. Although I would not go so far as the *Photoplay* (December, 1920) comment that "it is the most gruesome tragedy the screen has known," it is, without question, silent drama at its best.

Marc MacDermott, a graduate of the Edison Company returning to the screen after a long absence, gives the finest performance of his career as Peter, "the paralytic, who only sees and hears—whose eyes are his power of speech—whose son is his world and—his heaven." Using no facial expression, no movement except for his eyes, MacDermott demonstrates the consummate art of silent screen acting.

All in all, *While New York Sleeps,* with its three distinct stories and its three stars portraying three very different roles, must qualify as one of the greatest dramatic films of the silent era. With reason, contemporary critics compared it to *Broken Blossoms.* Its director, Charles J. Brabin, best remembered as the husband of Theda Bara, is here indicated as a director and screenwriter of considerable talent. (*A. S.*)

Above: *The woman and her first husband in "A Story of the Suburbs": "Is that hubby two on the line?"* Below: *The former vamp and the ex-detective in the final scene from the "Gay White Way" story.*

Above: "A Tragedy of the East Side": Peter, Buck, and Nina. Below: "A Tragedy of the East Side": Ned dies on the lap of his paralytic father.

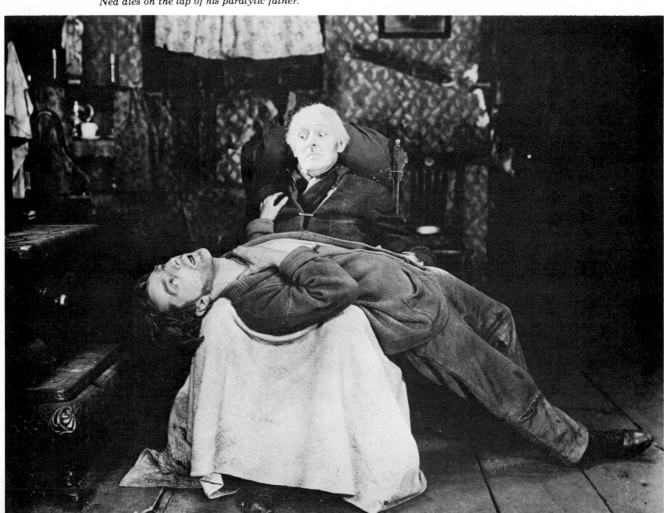

THE PENALTY

A Goldwyn "Eminent Authors" production. Released November 15, 1920. 7 reels (6,730 ft.).

Director: Wallace Worsley. Screenplay: Charles Kenyon (based on the novel by Gouverneur Morris). Photography: Don Short. Film Editor: Frank E. Hull.

CAST: Lon Chaney (*Blizzard*); Ethel Grey Terry (*Rose*); Charles Clary (*Dr. Ferris*); Claire Adams (*Barbara*); Kenneth Harlan (*Wilmot*); James Mason (*Frisco Pete*); Edouard Trebaol (*Bubbles*); Milton Ross (*Lichtenstein*).

SYNOPSIS: Blizzard, underworld king, cherishes mighty and undying hatred for Dr. Ferris, a surgeon who, because of a mistaken diagnosis, amputated his legs as a child. Rose, a Secret Service agent sent to spy upon Blizzard, falls in love with him. Posing for a statue of Satan by Ferris' daughter Barbara, Blizzard decoys her fiancé Dr. Allen to the studio, then, holding Barbara as hostage, demands that Ferris amputate Allen's legs and graft them upon him. Ferris seems to agree, but when Blizzard comes out of the ether, he finds that Ferris has instead performed an operation on his brain which has made a new man of him. He marries Rose but is soon murdered by a former henchman.

COMMENTARY: If *The Miracle Man* made a star of Lon Chaney, it was *The Penalty* that established his permanent claim to such stardom. For the first time, all the classic ingredients of a Lon Chaney "horror" production were introduced—mutilation, revenge, mental anguish created by physical deficiency, etc.—and it is doubtful that any later Chaney picture was better directed or constructed. *The Penalty,* production values aside, is decidedly superior to *The Hunchback of Notre Dame* or *The Phantom of the Opera.* Its story line and direction were not bettered by the more famous and lauded Tod Browning productions of a few years later.

Lon Chaney's presence dominates the film. It is hard to keep one's eyes away from his legs, or rather stumps, with the lower legs strapped back against the thighs. One can feel the pain that Chaney must be experiencing in perfecting that makeup, one braces oneself for the jolt as he descends down the pole to his underworld hideout, and yet no pain is ever visible in Chaney's face. The face exudes venom and hatred; bitterness is written all over it. As he poses for the bust of Satan, absolute malevolence is there. Malicious glee lights it up as he plots to rob the government bank and later to graft the legs of the fiancé of the girl he loves onto his own pitiful stumps. Warmth shines through only twice; as, in anticipation of his role in *The Phantom of the Opera,* he plays the piano—music ever soothes the tortured mind—and in the final, somewhat dubious, sequence after the brain tumor has been removed. It is Lon Chaney's film, and the supporting players matter little, although James Mason, as always, provides a splendid characterization of the weak, cowardly, villainous henchman.

Contemporary critics were surprisingly unmoved by *The Penalty.* In *Motion Picture Classic* (February, 1921), Frederick James Smith wrote, "We do not mind constructive unpleasantness, but this is clap-trap magazine thriller goo." Burns Mantle, in *Photoplay* (February, 1921), thought it "as cheerful as a hanging—and as interesting." J. S. Dickerson wrote in *Motion Picture News* (November 27, 1920): "The whole idea is wildly improbable, the romance connected with it inconsequential, and its multitude of characters get lost in condensing the book into feature picture length."

But here is a case in which the critics were obviously unprepared for this first screen excursion into that peculiar world of horror which Lon Chaney created and no one since has duplicated. It is unfortunate that modern audiences are all too likely to judge director Wallace Worsley and Lon Chaney by their other joint effort, *The Hunchback of Notre Dame,* and ignore *The Penalty,* a film which had he made no other should have ensured Chaney of screen immortality. (*A. S.*)

Blizzard terrorizes the girls who work in his "sweatshop," a front for his illegal operations.

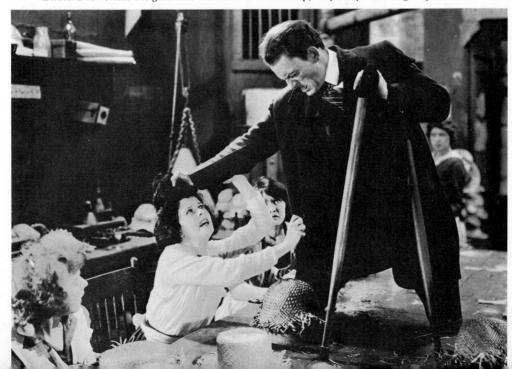

Above: *Blizzard with Rose, a government spy who falls in love with the man she has been sent to gather evidence against.* Below: *Blizzard poses for a statue of Satan, sculptured by Dr. Ferris' daughter Barbara.*

Above: *Blizzard and Ferris with the statue of Satan: "Mr. Blizzard, I am always at your service—but I must ask you not to return here again." Below: Blizzard, "the monarch of the Barbary Coast,"* *returns to his underground headquarters while Frisco Pete looks on.*

THE MARK OF ZORRO

A Douglas Fairbanks Pictures Corporation production. Released by United Artists, December 5, 1920. 8 reels.

Producer: Douglas Fairbanks. Director: Fred Niblo. Screenplay: Elton Thomas [Douglas Fairbanks] (based on an "All Star Weekly" novel, *The Curse of Capistrano,* by Johnston McCulley). Photography: William McGann and Harry Thorpe. Art Director: Edward Langley.

(The character of Zorro was also featured in the films *Don Q, Son of Zorro* [1925], *The Bold Caballero* [1937], *Zorro Rides Again* [1937], *Zorro's Fighting Legion* [1939], *The Mark of Zorro* [1940], *Zorro's Black Whip* [1944], *The Ghost of Zorro* [1949], *The Sign of Zorro* [1960], *Zorro and the Three Musketeers* [1962], and *The Erotic Adventures of Zorro* [1972], and in the television series *Zorro* [1957–1959].)

CAST: Douglas Fairbanks (*Don Diego Vega/Señor Zorro*); Noah Beery (*Sergeant Gonzales*); Charles Hill Mailes (*Don Carlos Pulido*); Claire McDowell (*Doña Catalina*); Marguerite de la Motte (*Lolita*); Robert McKim (*Captain Juan Ramon*); George Periolat (*Governor Alvarado*); Walt Whitman (*Fray Felipe*); Sydney De Grey (*Don Alejandro*); Tote Du Crow; Charles Stevens.

SYNOPSIS: In California of the 1820s, where oppression and injustice are rampant, a foppish, effete nobleman named Don Diego Vega avenges wrongs, disguised as Zorro, a masked man who marks his enemies with a "Z." As Vega, he is ordered by his father to court Lolita, but it is as Zorro that he falls in love with her. After various injustices, including the jailing of Lolita and her parents for treason and the whipping of a Franciscan monk, the noble-born caballeros join Zorro in freeing California from its corrupt governor and his henchman, Ramon. Zorro is unmasked and is able openly to declare his love for Lolita.

COMMENTARY: "Fairbanks' success," wrote Julian Johnson in the September, 1916 issue of *Photoplay,* "has been in his assumption of brisk American boys who were blind to obstacles, deaf to the quavering voice of fear, ready with the left hook, strong for chicken garnished with marriage license, and constantly, completely ablink in dazzling smiles." Johnson's statement fairly accurately sums up Fairbanks' early work in films, such as *Flirting with Fate, His Picture in the Papers,* and *A Modern Musketeer.* However, with *The Mark of Zorro,* the star's thirtieth feature and his fourth for the newly formed United Artists, the Fairbanks film career made a drastic change; Fairbanks the all-American boy became Fairbanks the swashbuckler.

The Mark of Zorro was the prototype for the Fairbanks features of the Twenties, such as *Robin Hood, The Black Pirate, The Gaucho,* and *The Iron Mask.* As such, its importance cannot be overestimated. In the chase through the

Don Diego Vega disgusts Sergeant Gonzales with his childish humor.

village toward the close of the film, Fairbanks displays all the stunts, climbs, leaps, and rope swinging that he was to repeat in different costumes and different time periods in all the films to come. Without question, it is the most entertaining of the actor's early films, but that is not to say it is a great motion picture.

The direction, as one had come to expect from Fred Niblo, is dull and static. The acting is restrained, but unimpressive, and the presence of two such accomplished screen villains as Robert McKim and Noah Beery counts for little. It is Fairbanks, and Fairbanks alone, who dominates the production. From his first entrance, as Don Diego Vega, hiding coyly behind an umbrella, audiences are aware that here is a new Fairbanks. The suspenseful build-up to the first appearance of the actor as Señor Zorro adds to the effect.

Contemporary critics, while perhaps slightly resenting Fairbanks' desertion of modern America for a costume picture, welcomed Fairbanks' new character. In *Motion Picture Classic* (February, 1921), Frederick James Smith wrote, "Doug is the personification of youth and high adventure; he is the spirit of all the things you and I, out in the darkened spaces this side of the screen, have ever dreamed of being. He is Everyman as he would like to be, if he could break the shackles of the commonplace and the everyday." (*A. S.*)

Above: *Zorro's first fight in the film: with Gonzales and his henchmen.* Below: *Doña Catalina, Don Diego, Don Carlos, and Lolita.*

Above: *Zorro forces Captain Ramon to apologize for having forced his affections on Lolita.* Below: *Zorro, Lolita, and Ramon.*

THE KID

A Charles Chaplin production. Released by Associated First National. New York premiere: Carnegie Hall, January 21, 1921. 6 reels (5,300 ft.).

Producer, Director, and Screenplay: Charles Chaplin. Assistant Director: Charles "Chuck" Riesner. Photography: Rollie H. Totheroh.

CAST: Charles Chaplin (*The Tramp*); Jackie Coogan (*The Kid*); Edna Purviance (*The Woman*); Carl Miller (*The Man*); Charles "Chuck" Riesner (*The Bully*); Tom Wilson (*The Policeman*); Albert Austin (*A Crook*); Nellie Bly Baker (*A Woman*); Henry Bergman (*Lodging House Proprietor*); Jack Coogan (*A Man*); Lita Grey (*Flirting Angel*); Raymond Lee (*A Boy*); Phyllis Allen (*A Woman*).

SYNOPSIS: The Tramp finds a baby left by an unmarried mother in a limousine which is subsequently stolen by thieves. After first trying to put the baby into a carriage containing another child, the Tramp decides to rear the baby, while the mother has a change of heart and attempts to locate the car in which she left the infant. Five years pass, and the Kid has become the Tramp's assistant, breaking windows which the Tramp then repairs. From a doctor, who has unsuccessfully attempted to have the Kid taken away from the Tramp, the mother learns that her son is still alive and advertises for his return. The proprietor of the lodging house where the Tramp and the Kid live sees the advertisement and steals the Kid from the Tramp in order to get a reward. In vain the Tramp searches for the Kid, falls asleep and dreams of heaven. However, a policeman disturbs his slumbers, and takes the Tramp to the mother's house, where he is reunited with the Kid and becomes part of the household.

COMMENTARY: *The Kid* represents the quintessence of Chaplin's art. It illustrates the highest point that Chaplin reached in the development of his particular form of comedy. Introduced as "a picture with a smile—perhaps a tear," it demonstrates the comedian's perfection of the use of the sentiment, pathos, and drama from which he draws his comedy. The same ingredients were to be used in the years to come—the substitution of a blind girl for the kid in *City Lights*, etc.—but Chaplin never advanced, and never really needed to advance beyond the point he had reached with *The Kid*. In fact, some might even say he regressed with the introduction of naïve political commentary in his later productions.

Aside from the Sennett production *Tillie's Punctured Romance*, which starred Marie Dressler and not Chaplin, *The Kid* was the comedian's first feature-length film. He spent more than a year on its making, which was a short space of time compared to the years he spent in preparing some of his later films. Despite his advances in comedy style from the crudity of Mack Sennett, Chaplin still retained links with the melodramatic symbolism of the teens. At one point, a scene of Christ with His Cross is shown to emphasize the plight of Edna Purviance, "the

In an effort to rid himself of the child, the Tramp tries to persuade a woman that she is really the mother of twins. (It was comedy moments such as this that led Francis Hackett in "The New Republic" of March 30, 1921 to write that "from an industry THE KID *raises production to an art.")*

woman whose sin was motherhood." (There's a title of which Griffith would have been proud!) Yet in one sequence, in which the Tramp dreams of Heaven, Chaplin embraces a surrealism and a use of fantasy and dreams which the cinema was not fully to accept for another thirty years.

The comedy, of course, is pure genius. There is perfection in the early sequences in which the Tramp has the Kid breaking windowpanes for him to replace; the timing in the interplay between Chaplin, Jackie Coogan, and that fine character actor Tom Wilson as the policeman is impeccable. Typical of contemporary critical reaction was *Variety's* (January 21, 1921) comment: "Chaplin, in his more serious phases, is a revelation; and his various bits of laugh-making business the essence of originality. No better satire has ever been offered by the comedian than the introduction of his ragamuffin kid seated on a curbstone manicuring his nails."

It is fitting that the teens decade should close with *The Kid*. It heralded a new era in screen comedy, and paved the way for the sophisticated feature-length comedies of Buster Keaton and Harold Lloyd. The era of straight slapstick comedy was at an end, and the age of the master comedians, who wrote, produced, and directed their own films, had begun. (*A. S.*)

Above: *A classic pose: the Policeman, the Tramp, and the Kid. (Of Jackie Coogan, "Variety" commented, "It is almost impossible to refrain from superlatives in referring to this child.") Below: A scene from the Dream Sequence, in which the Tramp imagines a heaven peopled by his earthly acquaintances.*